T0323701

Cambridge Elements

Elements in Reinventing Capitalism
edited by
Arie Y. Lewin
Duke University
Till Talaulicar
University of Erfurt

PRIVATE EQUITY AND THE DEMISE OF THE LOCAL

The Loss of Community Economic Power and Autonomy

Maryann P. Feldman
Arizona State University

Martin F. Kenney
University of California

Shaftesbury Road, Cambridge CB2 8EA, United Kingdom

One Liberty Plaza, 20th Floor, New York, NY 10006, USA

477 Williamstown Road, Port Melbourne, VIC 3207, Australia

314–321, 3rd Floor, Plot 3, Splendor Forum, Jasola District Centre,
New Delhi – 110025, India

103 Penang Road, #05–06/07, Visioncrest Commercial, Singapore 238467

Cambridge University Press is part of Cambridge University Press & Assessment,
a department of the University of Cambridge.

We share the University's mission to contribute to society through the pursuit of
education, learning and research at the highest international levels of excellence.

www.cambridge.org
Information on this title: www.cambridge.org/9781009517201

DOI: 10.1017/9781009321853

First published 2024

A catalogue record for this publication is available from the British Library.

ISBN 978-1-009-51720-1 Hardback
ISBN 978-1-009-32184-6 Paperback
ISSN 2634-8950 (online)
ISSN 2634-8942 (print)

Private Equity and the Demise of the Local

The Loss of Community Economic Power and Autonomy

Elements in Reinventing Capitalism

DOI: 10.1017/9781009321853
First published online: May 2024

Maryann P. Feldman
Arizona State University

Martin F. Kenney
University of California

Author for correspondence: Maryann P. Feldman, Maryann.feldman@asu.edu

Abstract: Capitalism is a powerful engine that requires finance. Private equity is part of the neoliberal transformation of capitalism that has failed the average citizen and unleashed a tsunami of leveraged acquisitions that have destroyed entire sectors of our economy. Private equity (PE) is a powerful force that has moved from restructuring industrial firms to buying up just about any economic activity in local communities that has assets that can be monetized, without any consideration of the impact on the quality of life and well-being of the community. This process has been aided and abetted by government policy. The authors of this Element explain the workings of the PE model and the reasons it has been so profitable. They document the effects of PE on firms and communities by examining a range of activities that once had a local focus. They conclude by offering policy recommendations.

Keywords: private equity, local economic development, policy preemption, subtraction effect, finance

ISBNs: 9781009517201 (HB), 9781009321846 (PB), 9781009321853 (OC)
ISSNs: 2634-8950 (online), 2634-8942 (print)

Contents

Turning and turning
in the widening gyre
The falcon cannot hear the falconer;
Things fall apart; the center cannot hold;
Mere anarchy is loosed upon the world,
The blood-dimmed tide is loosed, and everywhere
The ceremony of innocence is drowned;
The best lack all conviction, while the worst
Are full of passionate intensity.

Second Coming, Yeats *(1920)*

1 The State of the Nation

Taylor Sheridan's series, *Yellowstone*, pits the Dutton family of cattle ranchers, who trace their attachment to the land back 140 years, against a group of private equity-backed real estate developers that want to purchase it and convert it into vacation homes for well-heeled outsiders. This struggle exemplifies a process that has been occurring in a remarkable variety of businesses, as private equity firms, who are financiers search for undervalued assets that they can purchase and quickly liquefy to extract capital gains. As we shall show, ways of life, workers, customers, suppliers, land, and, of greatest interest in this Element, communities – are simply actors from which to extract value. This is not innovation nor the realization of creative activity but rather the enrichment of distant investors and their agents. We explain how private equity (hereafter, PE) works and show that this destructive version of capitalism is the outcome of a long-term transformation supported by all three branches of government that has been catastrophic for our communities.

The American Investment Council, the lobbying organization for the PE industry, announced that in 2020 its portfolio firms directly generated $1.4 trillion of gross domestic product (GDP) which was 6.5 percent of US GDP (EY, 2021). PE portfolio firms employed 11.7 million Americans. Moreover, this number does not include all of the firms that have been previously owned by PE and later divested. Nor does it include the employees of firms that PE investors have laid off or who lost their jobs when the portfolio firm went bankrupt. Our contribution is not to expose the operations of PE. This has been done by Appelbaum and Batt (2014) and, more recently, Morgenson and Rosner (2023) and Ballou (2023a). We build upon their contributions and also Olson's (2022) book *Ethically Challenged* that studies the PE transformation of the healthcare system. Finally, Brett Christophers (2023) suggests that we have entered the era of an *asset-manager society* as PE activities of PE spread globally. We build upon their contributions to consider the implications for local communities and the ability of local government to meet the needs of their communities.

The PE investment and wealth extraction dynamic is being repeated across the United States and has even been exported to Europe and vulnerable developing countries. PE has become a powerful force that has moved from restructuring industrial firms to buying up just about any economic activity in local communities that has assets that can be monetized, workers that can be paid less, and customers that can be charged higher prices – all without any consideration of the impact on the quality of life and well-being of the community. Advantaged by the U.S. Tax Code and the favorable treatment of capital gains, PE has grown ever-larger in size, impact, and political power. In search of new sectors from which to extract wealth, PE has reached into healthcare, housing, retail grocery and food services, prisons, childcare and eldercare services, and municipal services such as water and sewage, fire protection, and ambulances. The PE model has developed a remarkable variety of strategies to generate high rates of return as fast as possible. The survival of firms that PE investors purchase and the intertwined fate of local communities is irrelevant.

PE practices challenge some of the founding principles of the US economy. We pride ourselves on having a decentralized political and economic system where local governments and communities can make decisions that affect their future. States were seen as *laboratories of democracy*, pioneering new social and economic improvements expressing the values and dreams of their citizens. Local communities traditionally had assets such as local hospitals, newspapers, retailers, developers, landlords, and professional services that could be drawn upon to develop creative solutions to local problems. Drawing on local capacity, problems could be addressed in creative ways to benefit the community. Communities that lose this capacity are no longer resilient and unable to respond to internal or external crises. The new and remote value extraction-driven acquirers of these businesses make decisions with no input from, or consideration of, the impact on the local community.

The rise of PE has paralleled the last nearly fifty years of neoliberal ideology and statecraft. While touted as promoting the rights of individuals and the sovereignty of local interests, this ideology has moved in the opposite direction: the empowering of centralized, delocalized capital, and a deliberate policy of breaking down the local and state legislative barriers to the entry of extractive capital and disempowerment of the local. Today, the ability of localities, cities, towns, and even states, to be purposive agents able to affect local economic development has been almost entirely destroyed. Local and independent businesses have been acquired by PE, not to build and invest, but rather to liquefy the assets, workers' jobs, savings, and pensions, and erode customer service and quality – all in the single-minded pursuit of financial returns. Originally used to break up large and bloated conglomerates, PE has evolved to cover a range of activities. Through a finance-driven extractive process, PE has moved aggressively into services, especially healthcare but covering the range of main street activity that was once interesting and authentic to the character of the local place. The landscape is increasingly homogenous with absentee ownership and a diminished local tax base. The result is that many communities have not only lost resources but lack the local institutions that are able to promote the interest of their residents.

Quite literally, the resources and identity that local communities built up are being liquified, extracted, and transferred to PE owners located in a few financial centers such as New York, Chicago, San Francisco, and Los Angeles. For the organizations acquired by PE, the locus of decision-making has shifted away from the community to the offices of PE investors motivated solely by short-term, financial-engineering motivations solely focused on maximizing their internal rate of return. The result has been weakened, impoverished local communities that have little agency.

A fundamental premise of the US federal system was that the individual could relocate to different states and locales, voting with their feet for places that had the amenities, public services, and taxation that suited them. Federalism, historically a strength of the United States, was expressed in the prohibition of interstate banking. State attorney generals had the ability to consider the impact of cross-state border business acquisitions, prohibit and prosecute the corporate practice of medicine, and design local building codes that would preserve history and an authentic sense of place. The neoliberal regime came to control the executive, judicial, and legislative branches and actively worked to create a uniform playing field for the flow of capital. Rather than crafting policy responsive to local citizens, governments at both the federal and state levels have worked to favor the needs of large firms. The centralization of capital has resulted in federal and state governments working to restrict agency on the part of local governments seeking to respond to their unique economic situations.

American capitalism today is driven primarily by short-term profits rather than a desire to increase industrial productivity and implement technological improvements to benefit consumers and society. The United States is increasingly dependent upon other countries to smelt the steel for our bridges, make our semiconductors, produce batteries for electrical vehicles, build a modern train system, or even provide innovative housing solutions. Inequality has reached Dickensian proportions, as so aptly captured in Kingsolver's (2022) novel, *Demon Cooperhead*. In contrast, the sheer volume of wealth that PE firm owners have captured has allowed them to invest in our politicians. More importantly, this wealth has been used to reshape the judicial and regulatory system to increase PE profitability and reduce accountability, making it even easier to extract wealth without any reciprocal contribution to productivity or community well-being.

The rise of PE coincides with increasing income inequality in the United States. The differences between Americans in terms of their income and wealth have grown (Horowitz et al., 2020). One widely used measure compares the ratio of the income of the top 10% of earners in the United States compared to the income of the bottom 10%. From 1980 to 2021, the ratio had increased by almost 50 percent, with income in the top decile was $ 211,956 while the lowest decile was $15,660 (US Census Bureau, 2023). Another widely used measure is the Gini coefficient, which compares the equal distribution of income against the actual distribution, ranging from 0, which is perfect equality to 1, which is complete inequality, the Gini coefficient in the United States was 0.49 in 2023 (World Population Review, 2023). This was significantly higher than in any other G-7 country. The United States is inching closer to the level of inequality observed in countries such as India (0.495). Regional income disparities have also increased (Feldman et al., 2021), resulting in very different life experiences based on an individual's location at birth (Chetty et al., 2014). Communities have been described as *places left behind,* with questions about their long-term viability (Rodriguez-Pose, 2018).

The cause of the rise in economic inequality in the United States is frequently attributed to technological change, globalization, the decline in the returns of productivity to labor (including the decline of unions and the eroding value of the minimum wage), and the erosion of the social safety net. Certainly, all these factors are at work but they are all connected with the neoliberal regime that reaches its quintessence in the practice of PE. Our purpose is to document the central role of PE as a force degrading local communities.

While Appelbaum and Batt (2014), Morgenson and Rosner (2023), and Ballou (2023a) convincingly described the impacts of PE on the US economy and polity, it is remarkable that few have highlighted that these impacts are most acutely realized in local communities. The impacts of PE operations on local communities are largely ignored, even as economists have produced an enormous literature on how technology and globalization have affected local economies. One claim for technology and globalization is that the benefit we garnered from the loss of jobs was lower prices – the social costs were balanced by consumer benefits. New industries that were expected to and, to some extent, did emerge, were supposed to provide jobs in the new more sophisticated and higher value-added industries.

However, the PE industry is not interested in growing new firms or industries that could build productive capacity. The result has been a massive transfer of wealth. This has led to a withdrawal of economic activity in poorer neighborhoods in cities and small- and medium-sized towns – no place has been spared. This has been accompanied by decreased consumer choice, increased prices, and often decreased quality. It is difficult to see any discernible benefits to communities. The impacts of the PE model on local communities warrant closer examination.

The expansion of PE and its impacts on communities is the outcome of an ideology that favored the short-term maximization of liquid value at the expense of any other concerns. PE growth was assisted by public policy responsible for a tax code that advantages PE coupled with the deliberate weakening of regulation and oversight and an increasing disregard for the interests of workers, suppliers, and communities. The result was a transformation of the US political economy to one favoring financial intermediaries purely focused on buying firms with the sole goal of extracting wealth from them. In the 1990s, pundits and scholars argued that we had entered a so-called "New Economy" (Webber, 1993) – few suspected that it would be an extractive era driven by financial engineering and public subsidies. An economy optimized to operationalize the Gordon Gecko philosophy that "greed is good" as its core operating principle.

This economy is the result of an interconnected set of developments that have been brewing since the early 1980s. First, was the acceptance of the ideology of Neoliberalism, ratified by the election of Ronald Reagan and endorsed by all presidents, Democrat, or Republican, since. This ideology introduced a new narrative of how the economy, polity, and society should work and led to what Gary Gerstle (2022), terms the neoliberal order. Neoliberalism introduced capital-friendly policies that deregulated not only capital markets but rather all regulations, lowered trade barriers and, through budgetary austerity and privatization, reduced the roles of government in the economy (outside massive increases in military and policing expenditures) except for example when the financial system verges on collapse. Deregulation became a goal in and of itself regardless of the consequences to the environment, labor rights, health, or even protecting the financial system itself.

Second, the ideology stating that the only purpose of the firm was to provide returns to their owners, the practice of extracting this value was normalized.[1] Rather than appreciating that firms were successful due to the contributions of workers, suppliers, consumers, and the local communities within which it operated; the emphasis changed to focusing on short-term gains that would

---

[1] The quintessential academic expression of this ideology was the work by Fama and Jensen (1983).

benefit temporary owners. Firms were conceived as bundles of assets whose value should be monetized in the strict interest of their owners. An important goal became to develop monopolies over goods and services. This would allow maximum pricing thereby extracting value from consumers – this was all justified by the Chicago School ideology that postulated that regulatory oversight frustrated the effective operation of the market. This acceptance made not only monopolization ever easier, but also increased evasion of other regulatory rules – anything that increased the return on investment was acceptable.

Increasing the return on investment would be pursued by any strategy available. The gains came from cutting costs, specifically cutting workers' wages, hours, and benefits, or by outsourcing or offshoring the work. Price cuts came from squeezing suppliers or even finding offshore suppliers – threatening existing and often local suppliers by demanding what became known as the *China price*. These strategies were turbocharged by the new digital technologies that allowed ever more careful measurement of productivity and decisions could be made algorithmically with no concern for the local context. These digital technologies were expected to increase efficiency, but the gains of this efficiency were not captured locally. Rather, local communities were impoverished – the technology was used to increase return to capital – all other values were irrelevant.

As the return on investment became the overriding metric, financial capital simply saw people, land, plant, and equipment as static assets to be liquefied to extract as much value as possible. Pensions, rather than seen as deferred payments for workers to fund their retirement, became pools of capital to be raided, liabilities to be offloaded, or reneged upon. PE purchased firms and loaded them with debt – the target firm was purchased with its own assets as collateral for loans. The result was risky leveraged takeovers that pumped up returns for the PE firms and their investors at the expense of all other stakeholders. A new term *financial engineering* entered the lexicon. This new practice consisted of evaluating takeover targets as a mathematical problem that was simply a matter of calculating how to liquefy assets, secure tax benefits, decrease costs (and almost always quality), and raise prices.

As Krippner (2005) demonstrates, the result of this new neoliberal order was that economic value was increasingly accumulated through financial channels rather than investments that would increase productivity capacity.[2] This financialization was not limited to current profits but was also used to acquire existing firms and restructure them either by breaking them up or using them

---

[2] Brian Judge (2023) argues that the move to financialization occurred in the late 1970s and early 1980s as a political response to inflation. "Financialization was not enacted out of an ideological commitment to 'free markets' but as a desperate and pragmatic response to a deteriorating political condition[s]."

as platforms to acquire yet other firms – in each case restructuring with the goal of extracting their value – much like a spider catches its prey, injects its digestive juices, and sucks out they prey's juices. Invariably, the PE firm searches for capital gains, which conveniently are taxed at a lower rate than other types of income.

PE began by acquiring industrial firms, but they gradually expanded their investments to the retail and service sectors and even to acquiring housing and rental property and extending into basic municipal, social services, and health-care. This unending search for new opportunities to extract value has now infiltrated every aspect of a local economy. In some cases, state and local governments even subsidized PE firms by providing incentives and tax abate-ments to secure these immiserating investments. Even these incentives were calculated as part of the overall return – for the jurisdiction providing these incentives the benefits were invariably transient. Many locations worked to create a business-friendly climate but rather than building relationships, these subsidies simply became another source of capital extracted and transferred onto the spreadsheets of the financial engineers.

Third, while productivity increased and the economy has grown, the gains have not been widely shared. Economists expect that productivity gains will translate into pay increases – that is a sharing of the profits from increased productivity with workers. But from 1979–2019, productivity grew by 60% while wages grew by 16% (Mishel, 2022). Bivens (2011) terms this *Failure by Design*, as corporate power advocated for policies that resulted in increased unemployment (except post-COVID), declining unionization, stagnant min-imum wages, and enforced contract terms such as noncompetes, that limited worker mobility. Another significant change has been the continuing increase in nonstandard employment, including part-time, temporary, and contract work-ers, who have precarious working conditions (Kalleberg, 2000). These employ-ment relationships reduce costs and are part of the PE toolkit implemented after taking over a firm. When PE began acquiring local businesses, hospitals, local doctors, dentists, and veterinarian practices, precarious working conditions were extended to activities that previously had been quasi-public operations. The result has been a loss of the local elites and self-employed professionals.

National statistics do not differentiate, for example, between a dentist's office owned by a local dentist and a dental chain owned by PE. However the type of ownership can have fundamentally different effects. After a PE takeover, a dental practice is transformed from a locally owned small business, where the dentist is the proprietor to become a paid employee (though they might have an equity position, the other employees of the dental office receive no such benefits). All decision-making autonomy is transferred out of the community to the headquarters location of the PE owner. Furthermore, the PE-owned operation is not bound by local norms, reputation, or even shame freeing the operation to charge what the market will bear, use "surprise" billing, and upsell with an eye to profit rather than patient care.

The result is long-lasting effects on communities. Nonlocal ownership siphons off capital resulting in less local resilience: reducing a sense of community and destroying unique and authentic attributes. After PE investment, healthcare professionals become contract workers, previous business owners become salaried employees and prior homeowners become renters, thereby making them less embedded in their communities and increasingly vulnerable to the vagaries of financial markets. Individuals have less resources to invest in civic and community activities. All that remains are shuttered factories and storefronts with the same national brand establishments among the debris.

PE investment decreases the local tax base by weakening the economic multiplier effect. A downward spiral occurs as the quality of their services deteriorates with a declining tax base. PE investors then purchase and assume operations of municipal services. Selling assets, such as water systems, created an opportunity for cash-strapped municipalities to receive a one-time infusion of capital (see, e.g., Ivory et al., 2016b). Once in place as a monopoly provider, the PE-owned firms invariably raise prices on their captive customers while often neglecting maintenance and decreasing service quality.

Third, digital technologies have played a role by facilitating absentee ownership and monitoring. Computers were a central enabling technology making possible the expansion of financial markets. PE firms employ sophisticated data analysis to discover targets for takeovers, monitor operations, generate efficiencies, and extract value. Without the information and communications technology revolution, the ability to monitor and manage distant portfolio firms would have been more difficult. These technologies are mobilized to facilitate and accelerate value extraction. The objective is to examine a company not as a going concern producing a product but as a set of assets that could converted into an income stream. For example, the land that going concerns such as a hospital, mobile home park, or college dorm previously owned is converted into an asset to be sold and leased back – the land is converted into a lump-sum payment in return for a revenue stream for the purchaser (Davis & Kim, 2015). The PE owners threaten local governments with closure in an effort to force them to pay "ransoms" in the form of incentives and tax abatements, and such payments are also calculated as part of the overall return. For the local jurisdiction, the benefit is invariably transient. For the PE firm, all of this is merely notations on the financial engineer's inexorable spreadsheets.

Most paradoxically, PE investments are funded by endowments for institutions such as universities, philanthropic foundations, and, most disturbingly, by pension funds serving governments or unions – the governments that lose local assets and the employers that become the targets of PE takeovers. In other words, these organizations may benefit with promised, but often not delivered, high rates of return from the extraction of value from the very assets upon which they depend. The sheer scale of these investments is staggering. For example, in 2021, US pension funds, many of which are public, invested 9 percent of their total assets or $480 billion assets in PE (Gillers, 2022). The scale of the commitments by pension funds is growing even as it has been shown that the PE returns from these investments are dropping (Hamlin, 2023b). The often-cited reason for investing in PE firms is that they can provide a higher rate of return than other investments (Barber & Gold, 2007), yet more recent research challenges these returns (Jacobius, 2023). The paradoxical outcome is that these institutions fund the destruction of the local communities where their universities operate, their philanthropies seek to assist with grants, and where their company retirees live.

In sum, rather than financing prosperity, sustaining local diversity, and promoting resilient economies, PE is draining our communities of their assets in a race to the bottom. Ever more of the goods and services we use are provided by establishments whose operations are entirely motivated by the drive to secure short-term capital gains – at the expense of the broader definition of stakeholders – customers/patients, workers, and local communities. This short-term extractive mentality has resulted in an economy characterized by ever-worsening service, longer waits, uniformity, demoralized workers, and frustrated consumers even as wealth accumulates in the hands of the few that use the power this confers to shape the system to open even more sectors to this extractive process. While our mainstream media celebrates diversity, equity, inclusion, and authenticity; our places of work, consumption, and healing are transformed into cash flow-generating financial assets to be managed to extract as much capital as possible – where their importance to financial stability and the identity of local communities is of no account.

Consider how different the US economy would look if the PE funds dedicated to value extraction had been invested in new industries and new firms, creating jobs and prosperity. Indeed, international trade is often scapegoated for the deindustrialization of America. Yet, in an ideal world, international trade would have moved onerous and routine jobs offshore replacing them with higher value-added industries and better-paying jobs. Instead, the last forty years witnessed a growing decline in investments to increase productive capacity and generate high-quality work.

In Section 2, we summarize the development of PE as a response to the 1970s US economic stagnation. PE's first targets were the conglomerates in the 1960s and then larger industrial firms, which were derided as not operating in the interest of their shareholders (Fama & Jensen, 1983; Lazonick & O'Sullivan, 2000). PE began with a leveraged buyout model motivated to unlock the value that was hidden within conglomerates. Newly formed partnerships such as Kohlberg, Kravis and Roberts (KKR) leveraged the value of the target's own assets to borrow money to buy these conglomerates and unbundle them into small and presumably more efficient operating units.[3] In the process, the new PE owners reaped enormous capital gains. These PE firms soon moved on to buying yet other firms, particularly in manufacturing contributing greatly to the hollowing out of the US economy that began in the 1970s and intensified in the 1980s. To increase returns, the portfolio firms were pressed to outsource and often offshore many corporate functions ranging from production to research and development. The result is a landscape dominated by often PE-owned warehouses and distribution centers, with little of the industrial specialization and local knowledge that made the US economy innovative. With a few exceptions, our economy shifted from investing to building businesses to the goal of securing a rapid return. Venture capital, a subcategory of PE dedicated to investing in new companies, is motivated to harvest returns rather than building sustainable companies attached to local communities (Ioramashvilli et al., 2023).

After documenting the emergence of PE as an organizational form, its operation, how government policy changes supported its growth, and the adverse impact on local economies, Section 3 explores the remarkable range of local economic activities that have attracted PE investment. The expansion in scale and scope of PE is extensive and predatory. Section 4 explores policy responses that could halt, and even reverse, the adverse impact of PE investment. The policy response must be multipronged, involving federal, state, and local actors, with a focus on reining in the incentive to invest in PE and limit the public subsidies that contribute to PE returns. This is not so insurmountable once one realizes that policy has aided the development of PE and, over time, constructed the advantages that have made PE so profitable for its operators.

---

[3] Many of them soon went bankrupt or were sold to foreign competitors.

2 The Private Equity Model and the Looting of Local Economies

The real reason that we should be concerned about private equity's expanding power lies in the way these firms have become increasingly adept at using financial gimmicks to line their pockets, deriving enormous wealth not from management or investing skills but, rather, from the way the U.S. tax system works. Indeed, for an industry that's often held up as an exemplar of free-market capitalism, private equity is surprisingly dependent on government subsidies for its profits.

—James Surowiecki (2012)

The underlying logic of the PE business model requires explanation. Obscured by arcane and complicated financial, legal, and tax terms, the basic idea is not difficult to understand. Finance is needed in an economy, and investors search for the highest rates of return adjusted for risk. Private equity PE, a catch-all term that includes investment bankers, real estate investment trusts, hedge funds, and others, is defined as any alternative investment class that consists of capital not listed on a public stock exchange. According to one analysis, PE had the average annual returns of 14.65 percent compared with the S&P 500, which had the average annual returns of 5.91 percent from 2000 to 2020 (Cambridge Associates, 2021).

An historical examination is required to understand the incentives and subsidies for PE. Rather than investing in new capacity, the PE model is predicated upon buying a business, liquifying its existing assets, cutting costs, shedding liabilities such as pensions, and pressuring suppliers to reduce prices with little regard to any side effects – the overriding goal is to increase the time-adjusted return on investment (Barber & Gold, 2007). The model utilizes sophisticated financial engineering to take advantage of arcane tax code provisions often originated by PE lobbyist-influence legislation, reinforced by legal decisions and obscure federal regulatory rulings made by officials who often have, or hope to have, connections with PE firms. The entire operation is fueled by leveraged debt financing provided through banks and subsidized by the write-off of interest payments. The business model focuses on generating the highest rate of return regardless of the fate of the acquired business or its stakeholders.[4] This section explores the operations of the PE model, and its development over time and documents how the process operates to extract wealth from local communities.

---

[4] For a further discussion of the operation of PE, see Appelbaum and Batt 2014, Chapter Two; and Ballou 2023a, Chapter 1.

The PE Business Model

PE is a form of financing that occurs outside of public markets, with the purpose of buying existing businesses. PE firms organize partnerships (also known as funds), in which the general partner (the PE firm) manages the fund's investment portfolio for the limited partners who commit their capital to a specific PE fund and have limited liability and no management authority. To become a limited partner requires satisfying a legal definition of a qualified investor, which includes wealthy individuals, university endowments, philanthropies, pension funds, insurance funds, and foreign Sovereign Wealth Funds. The fund is marketed to prospective clients with a prospectus that describes the investment opportunity with a limited life expectancy of about ten years.

The PE limited partnership institutional form was adopted from the wildcat oil drilling industry (Kenney, 2011, p. 1965), where it had been used as a way of organizing high-risk, high-return business ventures. The limited partnership format had many favorable features for both the general partners, the PE firm, and the institutional limited partners. The general partners raise the funds and invest in a portfolio of companies and benefit significantly if they invest successfully. The limited partners have no say in the specific investments and also are not responsible for the activities of the general partners thereby limiting their liability in the event of any adverse outcome.

As a norm, the general partners are compensated in what is termed the *2 and 20 fee* structure. PE firms make money annually through management fees, which are assessed at a certain percent (often 2 percent) of the committed capital. For example, a $1 billion fund charging a 2 percent fee provides the PE general partners $20 million a year in revenue. The limited partners pay this fee annually regardless of whether a PE firm invests successfully. Carried interest, often but not always, 20 percent, is a share of capital gains allocated to the general partners at the exit event and aligns the general partner's compensation with the overall performance of the fund. Carried interest is only paid if the fund achieves a minimum rate of return known as the hurdle rate, which sets a minimum standard for performance. For example, a hurdle rate of 10 percent means that the PE fund needs to achieve a return of at least 10 percent per annum to the limited partners before the gains are shared with the general partners. The tax code defines carried interest as a long-term capital gain for tax purposes and is taxed at a lower rate than ordinary income if the investment is held for at least three years. This is an important way the US tax code subsidizes PE investment.

Once a fund is raised, the PE firm acquires firms, or parts of firms, from which it believes it can extract more money than the investment cost. The limited partners receive a return on their investment when the PE firm engages in what is known as an exit. An exit can occur, in a number of ways, through a public stock offering, acquisition of the portfolio firm, in whole or in parts, by another entity, or portfolio company liquidation through bankruptcy. For tax purposes, the profits realized from the exit are treated as capital gains and are taxed at a lower rate than ordinary income. When the acquired firm does well, the PE fund does well and both share in the returns. If, however, the fund does badly, the PE general partners have no financial responsibility to return the capital to the limited partners (Fleischer, 2008). Finally, the capital gains are disbursed to the limited partners without being taxed – the limited partners then pay any required taxes.

While there are more than 18,000 PE funds in the United States with more than \$4.4 trillion under management and \$1 trillion of uninvested capital (Warren, 2023), the firms are highly concentrated in only a few cities. As Table 1, New York City is, by far, the center of the PE industry accounting for nearly 43 percent of the total capital of the top twenty firms. Notably, the majority of the large PE firms were founded after 1980 and have grown rapidly as demonstrated by their fund-raising success.

The Reasons PE Is so Lucrative: How PE Firms Operate[5]

There is limited transparency and almost no regulatory oversight over PE practices. PE is inherently less liquid than public equity or stocks, so investors expect higher overall returns from PE. However the stated rate of return is not necessarily the case as there are with few generally accepted standards and guidelines as acquired firms are often illiquid. There are multiple algorithms for determining portfolio-firm value and the PE firm may choose the one that best serves their interest and achieves their desired rate of return – which ultimately can only be known at the time of a liquidity event (Hamlin, 2023a; McElhaney, 2022). This lack of transparency makes it difficult for limited partners, regulators, and others affected by PE to examine operations and follow the money.

The PE business model creates minimal risk to the fund as it uses the assets of the acquired company as collateral for the loans to purchase the company. Thus, the burden of repayment is on the acquired company itself (see Figure 1). In a typical purchase transaction, the PE firm uses its limited investor's capital to purchase approximately 30 percent of the total acquired company's purchase price. This is known as the equity investment. The remaining bulk of the acquisition cost is financed by taking out loans on the acquired company's assets, that is, financed by debt – the leverage in the leveraged buyout. The bank may either retain the debt or, more often, sell it on to institutional investors. The acquired company deducts the interest paid on the leverage: This alone returned

---

[5] We draw heavily upon Appelbaum and Batt (2014).

Table 1 World's largest private-equity firms, headquarters, funds, and founding year, 2023

2023 Rank	Firm	Headquarters	5-Year Fundraising Total ($M)	Year Founded
1	Blackstone Inc.	New York City, US	125,612	1985
2	KKR	New York City, US	103,713	1976
3	EQT Partners	Stockholm, SE	101,660	1994
4	Thoma Bravo	Chicago, US	74,093	2008
5	The Carlyle Group	Washington D.C.	69,681	1987
6	TPG Inc.	Fort Worth, US	54,965	1992
7	Advent International	Boston, US	52,939	1984
8	HG	London, UK	51,046	2000
9	General Atlantic	New York City	48,696	1980
10	Warburg Pincus	New York City, US	48,534	1966
11	Silver Lake	Menlo Park, US	48,280	1999
12	Goldman Sachs Capital Partners	New York City, US	45,358	1986
13	Bain Capital	Boston, US	44,347	1984
14	Clearlake Capital	Los Angeles, US	43,697	2006
15	CVC Capital Partners	Luxembourg, LU	41,750	1981
16	Vista Equity Partners	Austin, US	41,500	2000
17	Clayton, Dubilier & Rice	New York City, US	41,082	1978
18	Hellman & Friedman	San Francisco, US	40,925	1984
19	Insight Partners	New York City, US	40,166	1995
20	Leonard Green & Partners	Los Angeles, US	39,645	1989

Source: PEI 300, Largest Private Equity Firms in the World. *Private Equity International.* June 1, 2023. Retrieved June 2, 2023.

Private Equity Business Model and Ecosystem

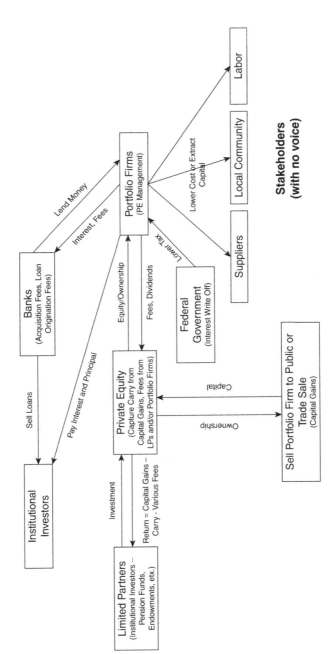

Figure 1 PE business model and ecosystem Adapted from Appelbaum and Batt (2014: 7)

between 21 and 143 percent of their investment to the equity holders depending upon the speed of the repayment and the tax rate applied to the interest deductions (Kaplan, 1989, p. 611).

The interest deduction is another way that the US tax code subsidizes PE investors. As is the case with the home mortgage interest deduction, this provision favors debt over equity financing. Here, PE investors took advantage of the original Congressional intent to encourage firms to take out loans to invest in expansion or capital improvement. This benefit was limited in the 2017 tax cut legislation to a 30 percent deduction of a firm's adjusted income (Wamhoff & Hughes, 2022).

Extracting Value from the Target

Upon acquiring a firm, the PE firm immediately appoints its representatives to the Board of Directors and initiates the process of reorienting the firm to a goal of extracting capital.

Often, but not always, a new executive team is appointed and members of the incumbent top management team are removed. The new executive team invariably receives large stock option grants to align their interests with the new PE owners. This equity share provides an incentive for the new management team to increase the value of the acquired firm.

As Table 2 suggests, there are a variety of tactics that can be employed to increase the value of the equity held by the PE firm. The most obvious is to cut costs through layoffs, replacing more expensive workers with less expensive ones, renegotiating contracts with existing suppliers, or finding lower-cost suppliers, often off-shore. Consolidating operations and closing facilities is another tactic.

Another way to increase the value of the acquired firm is to reduce balance sheet liabilities. Often, this is accomplished by renegotiating contracts and reneging on future obligations. For example, if the acquired firm has a pension plan, which is a liability, then ending or nullifying the plan can remove a large future liability, and, in certain cases, simultaneously provide access to the accumulated pension funds. Other liabilities that may be reduced include abandoning polluted sites or facilities that have dated equipment or challenging or repudiating outstanding legal judgments. The acquired firm's value is instantly higher when liabilities are decreased.

For example, Cobb (2015) shows conclusively that the takeover of a firm by PE investors leads to the termination of defined benefit pensions, thereby increasing the value of the firm and reneging on the promises to workers. A well-known example of this was the 1985 takeover of Revlon by Ronald Perelman and his termination of the company pension plan, which allowed him to extract more than $100 million in surplus pension value (cited in Cobb, 2015;

Table 2 Private equity strategies for securing capital return from portfolio

Decrease Costs	Decrease Liabilities	Increase Profits	Secure Subsidies	Acquisitions	Liquefy Assets	Payments of Firm to PE Owners
Cut wages and benefits, often through cutting hours. Use subcontractors	Shed pensions	Lower quality	State and local government	Develop industrial or regional monopoly Use to provide appearance of growth	Sell plant and equipment	Charge management fees to firm
Fire workers and managers	Close factories & facilities	Raise price	Interest on loans tax deductible		Sell real estate	Extraordinary dividends
Offshore work or inputs	Declare bankruptcy	Use debt leverage	Accelerated depreciation tax benefit	Economies of scale purchasing	Sell factories and leaseback	
Squeeze suppliers	Renegotiate contracts	Find lower-cost suppliers				

Schultz, 2011). This tactic is so popular that by 2022 there were few defined benefit pension plans left in the private sector firms.

In many of these cases, pension liabilities were transferred to the Pension Benefit Guaranty Corporation (PBGC), a government entity. From 2001 to 2014, the PBGC received $1.592 billion in pension responsibilities but because not all benefits are covered, over 100,000 workers or retirees lost benefits amounting to at least $128 million in anticipated retirement income. In keeping with the neoliberal ideology adopted by courts, a PE firm, Sun Capital, purchased, Scott Brass, leading it to file for bankruptcy, and then was allowed to withdraw from its employer pension fund without paying a penalty (Selbst, 2020). The legal system, despite various attempts by Congress to protect pensions, has been weaponized by the PE community against workers and, by extension, affecting the communities that depend upon the income from these workers to remain vibrant.

After PE investors buy a firm, there is an immediate pressure to cut costs to paydown the loans and increase the value of the firm – labor, quite naturally, is one of the costs. The academic research finds that after PE acquisition, on average, labor costs decreased by over 4 percent in the first two years. When PE takes over large publicly traded companies, job losses are far worse, about a 13 percent decrease in jobs in the first two years. While labor productivity increased by 8%, average earnings per worker fell by 1.7% two years post-buyout (Davis et al., 2021).

Another common tactic is to sell the acquired firm's real estate and then lease it back from the acquiring entity. For example, the portfolio firm sells its real estate and facilities for a lump sum adding the cash to its balance sheet. The entity that acquires the real estate and facilities does not have to be arms-length and may be a subsidiary or another firm in the PE portfolio. This capital can now be used to pay off the debt or provide a special dividend to the PE owner. The entity acquired by the PE firm, which has not changed location, is now saddled with monthly lease payments made to the new owners of their facility. The sale-and-lease-back strategy mentioned previously also benefits from the US tax code (Appelbaum & Batt, 2014, p. 79), which allows the portfolio firm to write off the lease payments as a business expense.

This strategy extracts the value of the fixed assets from the firm. In some cases, the portfolio firm may close facilities entirely, repurpose or sell them. Consider the case in 2022 when its PE owners closed the Delaware County Memorial Hospital in suburban Philadelphia: The real estate was too valuable as an asset to house a community hospital (Lapook & Kaplan, 2022). Real estate is only valued for the market price it can command – other considerations, such as patients' convenience, proximity to an emergency room, community health, or protecting the open prairie, are overridden by the drive for capital gains.

PE investors have developed many more complex strategies for increasing their returns. One of the increasingly common strategies is the "roll-up," the process of acquiring and merging multiple smaller businesses in the same industry into one larger consolidated company, which is better able to cut operational costs, and has an increased base of customers to drive revenue and thus can command a higher valuation than the parts. For example, PE firms have been purchasing all manner of previously locally owned small businesses, such as funeral homes, hospices, dental practices, addiction treatment programs, and childcare centers. The goal is to develop a dominant position in a local market, which will provide the PE firm the ability to cut costs by common purchasing, increase prices due to the reduction in competition, and/or rationalize operations by closing "underperforming" facilities.[6] This local roll-up is facilitated by US antitrust regulatory rulings that exempted purchases of under $50 million from having to be reported. If a dominant position in a *local* market can be achieved, then services can be curtailed and priced higher, and consumers/patients will have no alternative and must accept the new reality.

Ultimately, it is this short-term orientation to extract the maximum capital from their investments that weaken the acquired firms and wring cash out of the firm. If the debt cannot be repaid, the company, its workers, and its creditors bear the costs. The PE business model is a low-risk, high-reward strategy for PE firm partners. The result is a shell game with limited transparency (Protess et al., 2016).

There only have been a few attempts to track individual acquisitions to understand the outcomes. An example that has been carefully studied is G&H Orthodontics (G&H) of Franklin, Indiana, a designer, manufacturer, and distributor of clinical orthodontic products. G&H was acquired in 2010 for an undisclosed price by the PE firm, The Riverside Company. G&H soon threatened to leave Indiana and was granted $2.65 million in tax credits, property tax abatements, and subsidized worker training (McGuire Sponsel, 2022). After two add-on acquisitions that added "new product lines and distribution channels while adding new customers and cross-selling opportunities (Dorbian, 2017)." Seven years later, G&H was acquired by another PE firm, Altaris Capital Partners. Presumably, the state subsidies contributed to the value that the Riverside Company reaped. In another of the few studies of the impact of PE acquiring local firms, Olbert and Severin (2023) found that local governments' PE acquisitions experienced a 15% decrease in effective tax rates and a 10% decrease in total tax revenues. Indiana subsidized Riverside, and thus it is entirely possible that it paid to decrease its tax revenues!

Companies that are acquired by PE firms are ten times as likely to go bankrupt than a comparison group of similar firms (Ayash & Rastad, 2021). Brendan Ballou (2023a), in the book *Plunder: Private Equity's Plan to Plunder*

---

[6] We use parentheses on "underperforming" because the decision on what is underperformance is decided solely by the PE investor and can be an excuse for a business decision that is not actually related to performance, but rather some other financial consideration.

American, demonstrates how PE firms benefit even when the companies they invest in go bankrupt. Following the circuitous history of Friendly's Ice Cream, which was started in 1935 as a family business that grew into a 500-restaurant regional chain. When the founders retired, the business went through a series of different owners only to be acquired by Sun Capital, and then file for bankruptcy. After that, Sun Capital repurchased the company's assets – stiffing the creditors who had provided the capital to buy the chain in the first place! The financial gymnastics that Ballou (2023a) documents are truly breathtaking. When asked by *The New York Times* in 2012 about the failure of Friendly's and his arguable manipulation of the bankruptcy law, the co-founder of Sun Capital stated, "We don't make the rules" – a statement that is not entirely correct given the power PE has as a lobby.

Creating Private Equity – The Federal Government Paves the Way

The book, *Barbarians at the Gate* (Burrough & Helyar, 2010) is about the takeover of Nabisco by the firm KKR, which spun out of the financial firm, Bear Stearns. Many early targets were family-owned businesses that lacked a viable succession plan. These were often industrial concerns, and the focus was on restructuring the firm to sell in whole or in pieces in order to secure capital gains. With the change in ownership, long-standing relationships were no longer valued and the PE firms renegotiated existing contracts with suppliers and workers on more favorable terms. The targets of PE investment changed from dismantling the conglomerates of the go-go 1960s to the takeover and liquidation of undervalued assets in existing manufacturing firms in the 1970s and 1990s, to acquiring publicly traded companies and investing in consumer products and the healthcare sector – where the strategy is often to roll-up small entities in a sector into a larger entity that could exert market power. More recently, PE moved into acquiring municipal services. While the types of firms purchased and the methods for extracting value have evolved, the overarching goal, which is to reap capital gains, is unchanged. Given the incentives, it was probably inevitable that PE would enter ever more sectors in its search for monetizable assets.

Prior to 1970, institutional investors, defined as entities who make investments or manage large amounts of financial assets for pension funds, mutual funds, insurance companies, university endowments, and sovereign wealth funds, invested only small amounts in what was at the time perceived as high-risk alternative investment, preferring to hold equities in established firms and highly rated bonds. With the stock market crash in 1973–1974 and the collapse of several union pension funds due to misappropriation of funds, the Employment Retirement Investment Security Act (ERISA) was passed. The law charged the U.S. Department of Labor (DoL) with over-seeing pension funds. Pension fund managers were concerned that if they invested in firms such as PE that made high-risk investments, they could be accused of violating the so-called *prudent man standard* that protected them from being sued by their beneficiaries. Given the enormous losses that investors had absorbed with the collapse of the stock market bubble of the late 1960s and early 1970s, few institutional investors wished to be charged with being imprudent. The result was an almost immediate cessation of institutional funds flowing into alternative investments, such as PE.

In response to this drought, venture capitalists, who had recently formed the fledgling National Venture Capital Association (NVCA) began lobbying the Department of Labor (DoL) to loosen their interpretation of ERISA to allow pension funds to invest in what came to be known as *alternative assets* that invested in a portfolio of high-risk firms rather than a single high-risk firm (Kenney, 2011). In response to the lobbying, in 1979, the Department of Labor (DOL) issued an interpretation stating that pension funds investing a small portion of their total assets in entities that assembled a portfolio of high-risk investments such as a PE fund might do was not, in of itself, imprudent. The idea was that while each investment might be risky, the high returns from successes could mitigate the overall risk. This cleared the way for pension funds, public and private, and other institutional investors to invest in PE making ever-increasing amounts of capital available to PE firms.

Furthermore, in 1975, compensation for stock brokers changed from fixed fees to negotiable commissions. Reich (1989) reports that Wall Street revenues plunged $600 million, prompting a search for new sources of earnings that were paid during acquisitions and placement of the debt used to fuel leveraged buyouts. The ideology and operations of PE were perhaps best satirized in the 1987 movie *Wall Street* where the antagonist, Gordon Gecko, who made money from acquiring and dismantling companies, stated that the prevailing theme in "corporate America was survival of the unfittest" and that the solution to this was "greed" which was "good." Going further, he said he was not "a destroyer of companies, rather he was a liberator" – freeing capital to be used more productively elsewhere. The plot of the movie, which is drawn from the PE-organized leveraged buyout deals of the 1980s, was for Gordon Gecko to acquire a firm, Bluestar Airlines, expand it by using savings from union concessions and accessing cash in the firm's overfunded pension plan and then dissolve the firm leaving the entire Bluestar staff unemployed and with underfunded pensions and the communities where Bluestar employees lived, worked and spent their wages impoverished.

The growth of PE accelerated with the appointment of individuals who came from Wall Street to the Securities and Exchange Commission (SEC), where they advocated for deregulation and practices that benefited PE. For example, in 1982 the SEC adopted Rule 10b-18, which allowed stock buybacks (Lazonick, 2023). Corporate executives became motivated to ensure that stock prices remained high as stock options became a preferred form of compensation. Rather than paying dividends which were taxed as ordinary income, gains from stocks are taxed at the lower capital gains rate.

These significant changes are built on other precedents. In 1978, President Jimmy Carter signed a bill cutting capital gains taxes to 28 percent from the prevailing income tax rate of 49 percent. President Reagan would later cut the capital gains tax rate to 20 percent. The most visible lobbyists for this capital gains tax cut were from the National Venture Capital Association, which also included some individuals who would later shift from focusing on startups to the financial engineering that characterizes PE (Kenney, 2011). This cut was of particular benefit to PE general partners as their fee income was defined as capital gains that were taxed at the far lower capital gains tax rate instead of the higher ordinary income rate. Of course, this change also favored capital gains over wages, dividends, and interest that would be taxed as the higher ordinary income rate.

The term neoliberalism was coined at a Paris meeting in 1938, where Ludwig von Mises and Friedrich Hayek, exiles from Austria, vilified social democracy, as exemplified by Franklin Roosevelt's New Deal. Later, Milton Friedman would codify a new purpose for business as the Friedman (1970) doctrine in a New York Times article entitled *The Social Responsibility of Business Is to Increase Its Profits*. Under this ideology, businesses need only be accountable to their shareholders, shifting the prevailing view that businesses had responsibility to their workers, suppliers, and communities. This shifted the meaning of the term "investment" (Sayer, 2015), which had previously been thought of in terms of finance rather than as physical plant & equipment. This shift camouflaged the strategy of investing money in new wealth-creating activity towards the management of capital as a way of extracting value from underutilized or undervalued existing assets. While restructuring may be appropriate for some businesses, PE has perfected the practice of transferring the value of assets to themselves, thus removing any say over the claim of other stakeholders in the firms.

Neoliberalism was enabled by government actions. The courts, populated with neoliberal jurists assisted the expansion of PE firms. For example, in 1982, the Supreme Court struck down the 1978 Illinois *Business Take-Over Law*. The Illinois law required the material terms of a takeover offer to be made public, imposing a substantial waiting period to allow public comment and provisions for the conduct of a fairness hearing on the request of 10 percent of the owners of the acquisition target. The Illinois secretary of state could stop a takeover offer with adverse consequences. In the wake of the wave of leveraged buyouts in the 1970s, similar laws had been passed in forty other states with the intent to protect local businesses from takeovers. The courts prohibited what was seen as state obstacles to corporate control such as "disclosure-and-delay regulations that raise takeover premiums and lower the returns to acquiring firms. This takeover *tax* on bidders discourages investment in acquisition-oriented information and deters takeover activity" (Jarrell, 1983, p. 112). The court repeatedly removed obstacles and opened local markets to PE takeovers. This was not the only ruling in 1978 that would weaken local control over the financial sector. In that year, the Supreme Court ruled unanimously in Marquette National Bank of Minneapolis v. First of Omaha that state anti-usury laws capping interest rates did not apply to nationally chartered banks, effectively eliminating state interest rate caps (Judge, 2023, p. 149).

With the acceptance of neoliberalism at US law schools, the courts have almost invariably ruled in favor of the interests of private enterprise and finance capital (c.f., Cato Institute, 1985; Easterbrook, 1984). For example, PE firms were held to not be responsible for illegal or negligent actions of their portfolio firms since they own but do not directly manage the firm (Bonvino et al., 2021). In Ray v. Alad Corporation 1977, the California Supreme Court ruled that "apart from tort liability for defective products, . . . the acquisition of this manufacturing business imposed no liability upon it for [its predecessor's] obligations other than certain contractual liabilities that were contractually assumed . . . This insulation from its predecessor's liabilities of a corporation acquiring business assets has the undoubted advantage of promoting the free availability and transferability of capital" (Yamin, 1984, p. 257). This meant that the PE managers could push, if that was even needed, the firm's executives to increase returns with little concern regarding how this was accomplished. If there is litigation, the portfolio firm will be punished and, given the desire to exit its investments, by the time litigation occurs, the PE firm may no longer even be the owner.

The most important regulatory change of trajectory was the triumph of the ideology that supported industry consolidation by assuming mergers and acquisitions were neutral if they did not harm consumers. Rather than considering the impact on competition and market share, Robert Bork (1978) argued that antitrust should be about economic efficiency and that small businesses were inefficient and should not be protected. This ideology was predicated upon the belief that consumer welfare was promoted by the workings of their idealized market.

This interpretation narrowed the economic analysis used to identify whether a proposed merger was anticompetitive (Sokol et al., 2020). As the ideology took hold in the federal bureaucracy and the courts, to quote Lancieri et al. (2022, p. 5) there was "no matter where one looks, the overall downward trend in public civil enforcement of the antitrust laws is unmistakable, when targeting dominant companies that monopolize or attempt to monopolize markets. With some exceptions, government enforcement of the antitrust laws now boils down to enforcement against cartels and mergers that create (near) monopolies." Even when a merger was contested, the courts, led by the Supreme Court, rejected claims that it was anticompetitive, with the default assumption became that an acquisition was nearly always benign.[7] The weakening of antitrust law and the lack of enforcement attempts were a part of the greater context that was made ever more favorable to PE practices – especially their increased interest in local business acquisitions meant to roll up businesses and establish local market power.

In their quest for returns, any government program that can increase returns will invariably be exploited. For example, Woodall and Valdes-Viera (2020) estimated that 611 PE portfolio companies received nearly 16,000 CARES Act loans or grants worth at least \$5.3 billion. These portfolio companies were owned or backed by 113 PE firms that collectively held \$908 billion in cash reserves at the time of the request. The State Small Business Credit Initiative (SSBCI) was meant to be a historic investment in entrepreneurship, small business growth, and innovation. Through the American Rescue Plan, \$1.5 billion was provided to individual states to promote entrepreneurship meant to assist in reducing barriers to capital access for traditionally underserved communities (US Department of Treasury, 2022). To secure funding, states submitted plans to the U.S. Treasury – all with provisions for PE, further deepening their influence and subsidizing their operations.

State and local governments are often coopted into providing subsidies and incentives to retain jobs or facilities, often without any real long-term benefit. State and local governments offer tax incentives, sales, property, payroll tax credits and abatements, and infrastructure subsidies. There is a large academic literature on the limited economic returns to states for subsidizing PE – given their goal of extracting as much capital as possible before disposing of the firm. Due to the 10-year term of the PE fund, the emphasis is against making long-term commitments. The complexity of such subsidies makes it difficult to calculate their exact value. What is certain is that the net effect is to decrease state and government revenue, and, unfortunately, the promised benefits in terms of jobs and growth are rarely realized.

---

[7] As a result, the number of mergers increased, and the impacts have not been benign. Concentration has increased in three-quarters of American industries costing the average consumer \$5,000 per year (Philippon, 2019).

Buying Influence: Our Government and Private Equity

As the executive, legislative, and judicial branches of the Federal government have been restructured to produce a neoliberal society many have accepted the idea that PE invests in innovation and creates greater efficiency. This acceptance is encouraged by massive amounts of campaign contributions and the employment of government officials before and after service in government. As Table 3 indicates, the relationship between PE and politicians and regulators is characterized by a revolving door. *Open Secrets*, curates a list called the *Revolving Door* that tracks former government officials who moved from government jobs to PE, with the Carlyle Group currently employing thirty-one former government officials, while Blackstone has ten (Open Secrets, n.d.).

This movement is bi-directional as PE partners and managers run for elected office or are appointed to important government positions. The billionaire founder of Bain and Company, Senator Mitt Romney (R-Utah) is a salient example. When he ran for president against Barack Obama in 2012, the financial firm employees were thirteen of his top twenty contributors (Open Secrets, 2013). The current Chairman of the Federal Reserve, Jerome Powell, was previously a partner at the Carlyle Group. Given the enormous wealth that PE key partners have amassed, they are able to fund political campaigns, secure influence, and further shape rulemaking to favor PE activity. PE firms also make massive investments in lobbying. For example, in the 2021–2022 legislative session, there was an attempt to lengthen long-term capital gains time horizon from three to five years. Blackstone alone made campaign contributions over $40 million (Open Secrets, 2023a). The legislation was defeated.

In 2023, the principal PE lobbying organization was the American Investment Council (AIC), previously known as the Private Equity Growth Capital Council (PEGCC). According to some, PEGCC renamed itself because of a perceived image problem with the term *private equity*. Indeed, the PE industry was originally referred to by the name *leveraged buyout*. The practice of using a company's assets as collateral for the loan to take over the company was increasingly disparaged in the press, with calls for reform in Congress. The names have changed but the practices remain the same. Still, renaming and lobbying appear to have been successful as attempts to reform the preferential tax treatment on carried interest have not succeeded. The AIC retains a number of outside lobbying firms, making it difficult to trace activity and influence. Of the thirty in-house and outside lobbyists the AIC employs, 80 percent previously held government positions (Oprysko, 2022).

PE campaign contributions have increased with their reach into different sectors. PE firms are aggressive in activities with federal government procurement

Table 3 Revolving door: selected government officials joining private equity firms

Individual	Government Position	Dates Served	PE Involvement	Year Joined PE	Administration
			Executive Branch		
Tim Geithner	Sec. of Treasury	2009–2013	President, Warburg Pincus	2014	Obama (D)
Larry Summers	Sec. of Treasury	1999–2001	Managing Partner, D. E. Shaw & Co	2006	Clinton (D)
John Snow	Sec. of Treasury	2003–2006	Chair, Cerberus	2006	Bush Jr. (R)
Dan Quayle	Vice President	1989–1993	Chair, Global Investments, Cerberus	1999	Bush Jr. (R)
Colin Powell	Sec. of State	2001–2005	Chairman, Advisory Board, Leeds Equity	Unavailable	Bush Jr. (R)
William E. Simon	Sec. of Treasury	1974–1977	Co-Founder, Wesray Capital	1981	Nixon (R)
Arthur Levitt	Chairman, SEC	1993–2001	Senior Advisor, Carlyle	2001	Clinton (D)
Pete Peterson	Sec. of Commerce	1972 – 1973	Co-Founder, Blackstone	1985	Nixon (R)
George H. W. Bush	President	1989–1933	Senior adviser, Carlyle	Various year	H. W. Bush (R)
James Baker	Secretary of State	1989–1992	Senior Counselor, Carlyle	Various year	H. W. Bush (R)
Frank Carlucci	Sec. of Defense	1987–1989	Chairman, Carlyle	1992–2003	H. W. Bush (R)

Name	Position	Years	Private-sector role	Year	Appointed by
Arthur Levitt	Chairman, SEC	1993–2001	Senior Advisor, Carlyle	2001	H. W. Bush (R)
Mack McLarty	White House chief of staff	1994–1998	Senior Advisor, Carlyle	2004	Clinton (D)
Jerome Powell	Chair, Federal Reserve	2018 –	Carlyle (prior)	Late 1990s	Trump (R)
Kenneth Mehlman	Bush Admin. Various positions	1999–2004	Kohlberg Kravis Roberts & Co	2008	Bush Jr. (R)
Jacob Lew	Secretary of Treasury	2013–2017	Managing Partner, Lindsay Goldberg	2017	Obama (D)
Jay Clayton	Chair, SEC	2017–2020	Apollo	2020	Trump (R)
Leon Panetta	Secretary of Defense	2011–2013	Speaker, Carlyle	Various years	Obama (D)
Legislative Branch					
Evan Bayh	Senator, Indiana	1999–2011	Senior Advisor, Apollo	2011	Democrat
Paul Ryan	Speaker of the House, Wisconsin	2015–2019	Partner, Solamere Capital	2020	Republican
Pat Toomey	Senator, Pennsylvania	2011–2023	Board, Apollo	2023	Republican
Newt Gingrich	Speaker of the House, Georgia	1979–1999	Strategic Partner, JAM Capital		Republican
Joe Lieberman	Senator, Connecticut	1989–2013	Victory Park Capital	2014	Democrat

and reimbursement for services. These activities provide a captive market with guaranteed payment. For example, as the government mandated that health insurance firms cover opioid addiction treatment, PE firms rapidly began acquiring and merging opioid treatment clinics to take advantage of government-mandated opportunities, primarily paid for by Medicare (Chopra, 2018).

PE's political influence also extends to state capitals and local municipal government, with efforts to loosen consumer and worker protection. PE owns firms and service provider operations in every state and local economy across the nation. State and local governments who are trying to secure investments to keep and create jobs for their residents are easy targets and are willing to provide concessions (Olbert & Severin, 2023). Often there is limited transparency about specific deals. In sum, government actions, programs, and subsidies have been vital for the spread of PE to ever more sectors of our economy. The impact of PE is even more profound at the local level.

How PE Loots Local Economies

The impact of PE practices on local communities is profound. There are many reported cases where PE acquired a local firm, often a factory that was central to the community's economy and subsequently closed the operations, affecting the community and its suppliers (Alexander, 2017; Appelbaum & Batt, 2014). Data are available on the dollar volume of PE funds raised during the last forty years, yet the number of affected businesses and employees is difficult to trace. Even so, statistics tell us little about the impacts, particularly the cumulative impacts that PE acquisitions have on localities and their residents due to the relentless drive to lower costs and extract value from their portfolio firms.

One way to understand the impacts of PE activity in a location is through the economic multiplier effect, which measures the impact of money earned, spent, and re-spent in the local economy. To give an example, a dollar received by a locally owned pharmacy for the sale of a product goes to pay the wages of the pharmacy's employees and provides a profit to the pharmacy owners. In turn, this money circulates through the local economy to pay for other goods and services and in turn creates additional employment and jobs (Shuman, 2020). The multiplier effect is visualized in Figure 2 and demonstrates how a dollar multiplies as it moves in the community in a self-reinforcing circle. The more times a dollar passes between people locally, the more income, wealth, and jobs in a community. Staying with the pharmacy example, if the product is bought at a national chain or online, the owner's income is rerouted outside of the community, and the purchase no longer has a local multiplier. This is the logic behind buy-local campaigns.

Figure 2 Local multiplier effects

The takeover of a local firm by PE means that value will be transferred out of the local economy in two ways. Consider if a PE firm buys a previously owned local manufacturing plant. First, the PE owner will be remote: retained earnings and the securitization of the existing capital value of the real estate, facilities, and other such assets are transferred out of the community. Income and profits will be sent to the headquarters of the PE firm and the bank that holds the debt used in the leveraged buyout and no longer circulates in the local community. Second, in the search for greater efficiencies, the PE firms will likely fire employees, cut wages, trim healthcare benefits or pensions – extracting more income from the local economy. With new ownership, supplier relationships will likely change, and goods and services previously sourced locally are now sourced elsewhere, further decreasing the local multiplier effect. The reduction or elimination of this local spending decreases not only the direct spending but also the multiplicative impact of that spending. Moreover, the community becomes more vulnerable to economic shocks.

The loss of economic activity reverses this self-reinforcing process setting in motion a downward spiral. More than the direct loss of jobs are the indirect and unanticipated effects that erode the economy of a community. Recent research provides insight into the impacts of PE acquisitions. Samantha Zeller (2023) measures the impact of the PE hospital acquisitions on local healthcare insurance premiums from 2002–2017. Her research found that smaller local firms were adversely affected, with fewer new firms started and existing firms growing more slowly after the PE-induced health premium increase. In another recent study of PE hospital takeovers, Aghamolla et al. (2023) found that the increase in healthcare costs due to a PE buyout result in higher healthcare insurance premiums paid by local firms. These premium increases led to higher business bankruptcies, an increase in business loan volume, slower employment and establishment growth, and lower wages. These impacts are significant.

The extraction of value is a powerful blow to the local economy. With the loss of local ownership comes the loss of local leadership, with implications for the community. When the firm was locally owned and operated, it was part of the community, and the community influenced its decisions. Firm owners and executives often participate in civic decision-making and have a loyalty to the community. In contrast, PE owners command resources that allow them to offer higher prices. With a lack of other financing options, individual owners have every incentive to sell their businesses to PE, but any action that does not contribute to their internal rate of return is irrelevant to PE, as are the people impacted. And the corollary is that any decision that contributes to increasing the rate of return will be made, regardless of whether it impacts, or even destroys, a community. Without examples of how to run a business, and without access to local networks, entrepreneurs are disadvantaged in the places that need this activity most.

Local businesses and business leaders are often involved in philanthropic activities, supporting local organizations, charities, and initiatives. Business leaders have always played a central role in local networks and social structures. They are influential in building connections, supporting local entrepreneurs, fostering collaboration, and creating a sense of trust within the community. Local businesses sponsor local sports teams, hire local workers, and benefit the local economy through multiplier effects. When PE acquires firms, these networks are disrupted, and the community experiences a loss of wealth and fragmentation. When local leaders are displaced, the community has less social capital and connective tissue. The loss of local elites can result in a decline in cultural events and activities that contribute to the overall community quality of life, not only in small towns but also in large metropolitan areas (Lemann, 2000).

Moreover, businessmen are skilled individuals with specialized knowledge and commercial expertise. When they are replaced by employees, the commitment to the local community erodes. In poorer and rural areas, this can lead to a shortage of skilled professionals, and ultimately a decline in the overall talent pool available to support economic activities. Overall, the loss of local business leaders contributes to a stagnation of economic activity, decreased job opportunities, and often a decline in economic activity, associated with deaths of despair (Case & Deaton, 2020).

Section 3 describes the scale and scope of PE investments, demonstrating that nearly every sector of local community economic life is affected and immiserated by the extractive practices of PE investors.

3 Surveying the Demise of the Local

In earlier decades, most industries were fragmented with a large number of independent, small- and medium-sized firms. With the lack of antitrust enforcement, there has been an inexorable consolidation as large firms seek to dominate ever more industrial sectors. For example, the grocery store business was fragmented with a large number of smaller local and regional chains. In the last three decades, PE investors have actively sought to acquire and consolidate these smaller chains. To illustrate, Star Market, established in 1915 and previously family-owned has, in recent times, been merged or was sequentially acquired by Shaw Markets, J Sainsbury, and Albertsons, growing ever larger with every transaction, only to be currently owned by Cerberus Capital Management. These types of acquisitions, which are repeated across ever more sectors, create local monopolies (Kuttner, 2022), with all the associated behavior – price increases accompanied by an indifference to quality. Not satisfied with normal rates of return, the PE owners may even drive the operation into bankruptcy – if that is the best option to extract the maximum value from the portfolio firm. But what is viewed as an asset from which to extract the maximum value may be an essential activity to a local community, providing much-needed goods and services as well as jobs. The impacts on local residents can be devastating as customers and patients may have to travel further to secure food and services. Daily tasks become onerous, and people may decide that living in the town is no longer viable.

Consider that PE began by purchasing conglomerates through leveraged buyouts and dismantling them by spinning off their disparate divisions. Demonstrating high rates of return and receiving large infusions of capital, PE firms searched for additional opportunities and thus began their infiltration into everyday local life through investing in a remarkable range of business activities. This dynamic is particularly visible in healthcare, where PE investments have come to dominate activities including in ambulance services, specialty medical practices, emergency rooms, hospitals, clinics, and nursing homes, among others. Arguably, PE may have added value by breaking up large industrial conglomerates or increasing efficiency in lagging sectors. However, the application of the PE model to essential goods and services such as healthcare seems far more dangerous.

This section documents how PE firms have evolved, applying their investment model to ever more sectors, affecting Americans from cradle to grave – daycare to funeral homes. These sectors are attractive for PE investment because they are essential and often recession-proof. Consumers are willing to pay handsomely, and perhaps even more importantly government and insurance provide apparently limitless pockets. PE has taken over a range of previously local business areas that were once fragmented, consolidating them into a larger company to build brand name recognition, decrease operational costs, and develop monopoly or oligopoly positions to increase revenue. This *roll-up strategy* is being used in diverse sectors such as retail, housing, dental practices, and veterinary clinics. Even activities such as car washes and bowling alleys are not immune.

It Began with Manufacturing

The original application of the PE model was targeted towards manufacturing firms through LBOs. One early iconic LBO was KKR's purchase of the machinery conglomerate Houdaille Industries in 1978 (Appelbaum & Batt, 2014, pp. 25–27; Holland, 1989), which, after PE firms had drained the firm, went bankrupt to the detriment of its workers, retirees, the local community, and US competitiveness. The role of PE acquisitions and restructuring is amply described in academic articles,[8] the popular press, and even full books as firm after firm succumbed to takeover offers (Baker, 1992; Holland, 1989). Initially, the targets were conglomerates that were perceived to be under-valued by the stock market. After the acquisition, the various businesses were spun off under the assumption that they would be more efficient if operating separately. Of course, the tax benefits that undergirded these financial actions are not efficiencies – they are subsidies that benefit the PE firm. What these initial LBOs did demonstrate was the feasibility of this type of investing.

Given their success with breaking up conglomerates, PE investors shifted their practice to the purchase of undervalued US manufacturing, leveraging the firms' own assets in the takeover. The PE investors invariably applied their regime of extreme cost-cutting, ditching liabilities such as pension obligations and environmental cleanup, renegotiating contracts with workers and suppliers, and lowering quality. Part of cost-cutting was offshoring production wherever possible. This new phase of PE targeting would have a far greater impact on the communities where factories were downsized or closed. In aggregate, PE played an important role in the destruction of the towns and cities of what is now known as the Rust Belt. The impacts were most significant for local communities that were dependent on one major employer. Brian Alexander (2017) describes what happened to Lancaster, Ohio after PE firms repeatedly bought and sold Anchor Hocking until the point where the firm and its local operations were closed. At the end of this process, this economic anchor for Lancaster had disappeared, and it was one more devastated Rust Belt city. PE firms repeated this practice across the industrial Midwest, as the factories were closed, and pension plans were destroyed. Facilitated by tax law and other mechanisms such as NAFTA, the offshored jobs were never

---

[8] Many of the articles in the business and finance literature treat profitability as the sole issue and do not even consider the costs to other stakeholders. The earliest critiques of the LBO/PE model came from reporters who saw the real-life impacts. Also, the business school literature is remarkable in the sense that it often argues that PE investments are beneficial even though much of the so-called profitability comes from reneging on pension fund obligations and various tax breaks. The secondary effects on retirees and other taxpayers are not considered.

replaced. Though paradoxically, after forty years of these practices in 2023 the United States is concerned about its offshore supply chains – but few mention how financialization and rapacious PE investors contributed to the current state of events.

To illustrate how pervasive the phenomenon was in the decade of the 1980s, Zorn et al. (2005, p. 284) found that 144 of the Fortune 500 firms (29 percent), mostly industrial firms, were subject to hostile takeovers: 90 percent (129) were successful. An analysis of large acquisitions from 1983 to 1998 concluded that the PE acquisition shifted as the number of unrelated or diversifying acquisitions dropped dramatically, while acquisitions of firms in the same industry or firms that were suppliers increased. Same industry acquisitions increased market power, while the acquisition of suppliers captured control of critical components and removed their availability for competitors. In addition, the supplier firms were often relocated offshore as part of a more general trend that accelerated after China joined the WTO in 2000.

This early PE investment in manufacturing could be understood as a reorganization of declining industries for redeployment to new sunrise industries. Investing in new technologies and new firms became the focus of venture capital, a specific form of PE associated with the rise of Silicon Valley. The VC model relies on taking a share of the company ownership in return for active management with the objective of increasing the companies' valuation. Yet, investing in new technologies and building successful companies is risky and time-consuming, while acquiring existing companies using their own assets to flip and resell is relatively easier. Moreover, the amount of money invested in PE dwarfs the investment of VCs. VCs have a noted tendency to invest in certain regions and certain technologies, especially information technology and biotech, and overlook other sectors of the economy (Florida & Kenney, 1988). In sum, the deindustrialization of US manufacturing we have observed over the past forty years is no surprise given the modus operandi or PE investors.

From the perspective of the locals, the closure or downsizing of a local manufacturing operation after PE equity devastates the affected community. However, PE firms and their practices were evolving and finding new sectors. More recently, PE has become pervasive, with activity in every community and through purchasing existing local businesses resulting in an octopus-like grasp on a range of its acquisitions in the average community. Our analysis relies on existing studies and reports. As a reality check, using a well-known proprietary investment data source, we counted sixty-three separate PE investments made in one small American city since 2000. Indeed, all the activities we discussed were targets in this city.

Extracting Wealth from the Healthcare System

... when the fundamental characteristics of the private equity business model are combined with the unique structure of the United States healthcare market, the results are potentially catastrophic for patients, payers, and the long-term stability of the healthcare supply chain. And, because the consequences in healthcare involve not just dollars but lives, these potential harms must not be ignored.

Scheffler et al. (2021)

PE investment in the healthcare industry is dramatically weakening local communities and contributing enormously to the evolution of an overly expensive, badly performing system that leaves neither healthcare professionals nor patients and their families happy (Olson, 2022).[9] Beginning in the 1990's PE brought its form of investing to an ever-increasing variety of healthcare-related areas exploiting the fact that these services are not only essential but they are also covered by Medicare and private insurance making healthcare very lucrative. This trend coincides with healthcare becoming an ever-larger share of the US economy, increasing from 12.1% in 1990 to 18.3% in 2021 of GDP. The total size of the US healthcare market is $808 billion, with 65 percent or the lions' share of revenue coming from patient care, where PE investment has been aggressive. In 2010, the estimated annual PE deal value was $41.5 billion – in 2021 it had grown to more than $200 billion. The sheer scale of this investment is telling: PE firms have invested over $750 billion into US healthcare since 2010 (Scheffler et al., 2021). Even with Olson's (2022) vital work, the scope of PE ownership in the healthcare sector remains unmeasured.

By 2023, PE has penetratednearly every aspect of the lucrative US healthcare industry and is transforming them with the same playbook deployed in other industries – purchasing going concerns by levering their assets, saddling them with debt, and then decreasing labor costs, and raising prices. The income from the now-captive operation is funneled out of the local community to pay the interest on the debt and PE fees. Due to the multiplier effect, the community is worse off as income and profits accrue to the PE firm. But, even worse for the local community, control of decision-making moves away from the local community to the location of the PE firm, where, for example, healthcare assets are managed by accounting algorithms that constantly assess the income from each type of care, with local healthcare professionals pressured to offer or prescribe the care that generates the greatest return. In contrast to the local

---

[9] In the last five years, there has been a plethora of reports from various groups and editorials published in various specialty medical journals on the investment and impact of private equity in health care. Also, there has been an increase in academic studies of the phenomenon. From our perspective, the most comprehensive analysis of PE in healthcare is Olson (2022), but also see Scheffler et al. (2021, 2023). We draw upon their work extensively in this section.

hospital or doctor's practice that often provided pro bono work for the indigent, the PE owners have no interest or relationship to the community – they are simply a population from which to extract value. If the healthcare operations are not profitable, they will be closed as a purely economic decision that does not consider the healthcare outcomes for the local community.

Consolidating Hospitals into Systems while Dismantling the General Hospital

Traditionally, hospitals were operated by religious organizations, local government, local nonprofits, or as a university medical center. Hospitals saw their mission as operating for the good of the community and served as a center of activity and a place where individuals in need could get help. From the Roosevelt Administration through the Nixon administration, legislation increased access to healthcare by providing insurance and expanding benefits (KFF, 2009). This changed in the mid 1970s when the Carter administration began a focus on cost containment and divested oversight and administration to state governments. In response, individual hospitals consolidated into systems that typically involved similar-sized hospital systems merging or a larger hospital system acquiring a smaller one, often in the same city or state. The last decade has seen cross-market mergers – the merger between hospitals located in geographically separate areas. For example, the $27 billion Atrium–Advocate Aurora merger was completed in December 2022, creating the fifth-largest hospital system in the United States, serving nearly 6 million patients in the South and Midwest. Invariably, after these acquisitions and consolidations, managers with financial experience replaced doctors as hospital administrators.

In 2023, PE investors owned 30 percent of all for-profit hospitals (Private Equity Stakeholder Project, 2023), and they have begun making inroads with nonprofit hospitals (Becker's Hospital Review, 2013).[10] However, this dramatically underestimates the impact that PE investors have had, as it includes only those currently owned by PE, not those that it has bought and have gone bankrupt or been sold to other investors including the public. Perhaps the most celebrated hospital system acquisition by PE was the 2006 $33 billion (of which $11.7 billion was leveraged debt) purchase of HCA (Hospital Corporation of America), the largest for-profit hospital operator in the United States (Hospital Corporation of America, 2006). This buyout proved to be wildly profitable and became the model for PE investing in healthcare.

---

[10] This statistic is the percentage at a particular time. A number of private hospitals may have earlier been owned by PE investors and later spun off. Also, it does include the hospitals that were closed. Thus, the true number of private for-profit hospitals is surely dramatically larger.

The alleged "victims" in the HCA buyout were institutional shareholders as the PE firms that bought HCA were later accused of price-fixing the bidding for the firm *(Becker's Hospital Review*, 2012). PE investors were later accused in a series of *New York Times* investigative articles of requiring physicians to treat more patients and changing the coding for procedures to extract more reimbursements from insurers (Abelson & Creswell, 2012; Press, 2023).

Ultimately, the HCA acquisition was a success for the PE firm and the limited partners, yet the costs were born by the employees who faced increased workloads, the insurance firms, and the government insurer Medicare who faced increased costs due to the practice of *up-billing* by switching coding for procedures to receive higher reimbursement or the cherry-picking of healthier patients. Health outcomes after the acquisition of hospitals by PE are documented to decline, with many horror stories of abuse (Pearl, 2023), even as costs increase after PE completes an acquisition (Borsa et al., 2023; Schulte, 2022).

Hospitals provide an attractive investment for PE because consumers' need for health is recession-proof, decision-making and accountability are not transparent, and reimbursement from insurance is guaranteed. Hospitals hold assets such as real estate and equipment that could be leveraged for the initial purchase and then sold off and leased back. There are many studies and reports on the outcome of hospital acquisitions (c.f., Bruch et al., 2020), that conclude that social costs to communities and public health are substantial.

Hospitals stand at the heart of their communities and their presence contributes to community resilience and stability. In addition to providing clinical care for the ill and supporting public health, hospitals have a mission that includes caring for all members of the community, especially those most in need. Hospitals have traditionally provided emergency rooms, and continuing care for the critically ill, and are vital in disaster responses and preparedness. Hospitals are invariably among the largest employers in a community and provide a wide range of job opportunities for healthcare professionals, support staff, and administrative personnel. After an acquisition, invariably PE consolidates operations and often closes the local hospital – removing this key actor from the community causing many patients to travel great distances for care.

PE investors have engaged in the un-bundling, re-bundling, and outsourcing of the various functions and departments previously managed by the hospital. The general hospital as a unitary entity has been dismantled: noncore services from cleaning and food preparation, which were once often unionized, and medical-related services previously provided by hospitals have been outsourced. Even prior to the pandemic, there were shortages of medical professionals in the United States, but particularly concentrated in nursing. Bur shortages exist in many other medical specialties such as physical therapy and various technologists such as radiology, and ultrasound. There are ample reasons for these shortages that include criticisms of the general management, notably PE-owned hospitals (Bugbee, 2022, p. 6).

What is certain is that the healthcare contract labor industry is growing rapidly. We direct attention to nurses and physical therapists. Already prior to the pandemic, traveling nurse revenue increased from $3.9 billion in 2015 to $11.8 billion in 2021 (Bugbee, 2022). The cost to the hospital of a traveling nurse may be as high as $270 per hour, while the traveling nurse receives $85 per hour plus benefits including housing and meal allowances – the remainder is retained by the traveling nurse agency. These excellent profit margins attracted PE, as Bugbee (2022, p. 13) shows PE acquisitions of medical staffing firms increased from two or three per year in 2010 and 2011, respectively, to twenty-seven and eighteen, respectively, in 2021 and 2022. PE firms also began investing in online staffing platforms.

From the local perspective, traveling nurses from outside the community are only temporarily local, thereby having connections to the local community. Conversely, local staff nurses become traveling nurses due to the wage differential and are out-of-town for long periods and lose connections to their local economy. Not only do patients not develop relationships with ever-changing staff, care is more costly and profits are transferred to the contracting firm; many of which are owned by PE firms.

While the hospital can be understood as a core institution for community healthcare provision, the healthcare system has become more differentiated and complex – and at each node, one encounters PE investment consolidating and extracting value. The following section considers medical specialties (e.g., urology, dermatology, etc.) and emergency rooms where PE plays a major role through their ownership of contract management groups (Berry & Barach 2021).

Hospital Departments & Emergency Rooms

PE focused on acquiring organizations that provide hospitals with clinical services outsourced to control costs. The PE model is to purchase individual private medical practices, consolidate them into a bigger entity that provides outsourced services to the hospital, and then sell the entity for a profit. The most obvious rollup is horizontal by purchasing physicians' practices in the same specialty, with the objective of establishing market power. For example, after Medicare announced coverage for total knee replacements in outpatient settings, PE investors began rolling up orthopedic practices (Appelbaum & Batt, 2020, p. 52). Medical professionals are often among the wealthiest and most committed residents in a local community. The retirement of baby-boom generation physicians, coupled with the high educational debt incurred by newly minted doctors, has created an opportunity for PE firms to purchase practices and turn physicians into employees rather than small business owners, shifting the locus of control away from the local community and towards the location of the PE firm.

One single PE firm has more than 50 percent market share of full-time-equivalent physicians in 13 percent of American communities (Scheffler et al., 2023, p. 4). Price increases associated with PE acquisitions are exceptionally high where a PE firm controls a competitively significant share of the local market. When a single PE firm controls more than 30 percent of the market, the cost of an office visit increases by 18 percent for gastroenterology, 16 percent for obstetrics and gynecology, and 13 percent for dermatology. The PE firm may require the physicians' offices they control to order tests and procedures from other firms they own, guaranteeing greater opportunities for increasing revenues and profits – at the expense of patients, insurers, or the government. This integration of the supply chain is difficult to track and is rarely recognized when reporters or researchers examine the control PE firms have in a particular local medical specialty market.

The Emergency Room (ER) is one of the most vital hospital operations for a local community and has attracted significant PE attention: from 2009 to 2019, PE control grew from 8.6 to 22 percent of the total market (Adler et al., 2023), with other estimates as high as 40 percent of the market for ER services (Wolfson, 2022). There is ample anecdotal evidence that as a result of the sale by hospitals of their ERs to PE firms, the price per visit increased, while the quality of service decreased, as the PE firms reduced costs by replacing physicians with nurses (Kelman & Farmer, 2023) and used other cost-cutting strategies. Prior to the passage of the No Surprises Act in 2020, one of the largest income sources for PE-owned ERs was out-of-network billing that allowed them to charge wildly inflated bills for service. In 2023, the KKR-owned Envision Healthcare ER declared bankruptcy over litigation with health insurers regarding out-of-network surprise billing and upcoding of procedures (Halleman, 2023). As a result, in Texas, there are lawsuits to overturn the law (Pearl, 2023). The experience at the ERs is reproduced in nearly every corner of the healthcare sector. In the overall strategy to extract value, tactics include price increases, medical insurance up-coding of procedures, attempts to sell "add-on" services, lowering labor and other costs, service quality declines, and the use of leverage to extract value differ only by the specificity of each setting.

The original aim of outsourcing ERs was to lower costs (Appelbaum & Batt, 2020, p. 59). However, outsourcing the ERs had a surprising result, namely, the ER doctors were more likely to admit patients from the ER to the hospital. This benefited the hospital because, due to government policy, Medicare pays less for patients treated in the emergency room than those admitted to the hospital! This encourages not-for-profit hospitals to outsource their ERs. The ultimate result, of course, is that the hospital outsources its ER, which then experiences PE acquisition.

ERs are only the beginning. Instead of ERs, some of the traffic can be rerouted to outpatient urgent care centers, which are attractive to uninsured patients and medical insurers due to their lower cost and simplified organizational structures, which require less staffing and lower facility maintenance costs. Referred to as *Doc in a Box,* the typical center is small and located in a strip mall with one physician, one physician assistant or nurse practitioner, one or two medical assistants, one radiological technician, one center manager, and one or two receptionists. The services provided in these centers require a narrower range of skilled staff with less medical expertise, although perhaps, more social and patient communication skills. Employees are also paid less than hospital employees in similar occupations with similar educational and demographic characteristics (Berry & Barach, 2021). On average, depending on the occupational group, urgent care centers pay roughly 9–12 percent lower hourly wages than hospitals, except cleaning services (which pay 18 percent lower). Moreover, unionization rates in outpatient care are half those of hospitals – 6 percent versus 13.6 percent in 2015 (Appelbaum & Batt, 2020, p. 44). The Urgent Care Centers, while clearly useful, are changing healthcare.

The acquisition of ERs by PE means that one of the key community-facing healthcare activities would be now managed by the PE textbook. One result was a rise of "surprise billing," as PE firms strove to increase their revenue (Sanger-Katz et al., 2019) and, as every American who has used an ER knows, ever longer waits and overworked doctors and nurses. Moreover, ERs became a template for outsourcing ever more activities from the hospital, which we briefly discuss in the next section.

Outsourcing Specialties and Private Equity

The unbundling of the hospital fed by privatization and the possibility of accessing federal monies has moved forward inexorably both in terms of medical specialties and functions such as surgery, and kidney dialysis. This has been motivated not by greater efficiency in terms of the delivery of high-quality healthcare but rather by an ability to extract rents.[11] Rather, the goal of

---

[11] The general hospital model is effective in countries with universal healthcare that also have far better health outcomes than the United States. It is also effectively used by the Kaiser Permanente system that was a "private" response established by New Dealer Henry J. Kaiser. The academic literature comparing the Kaiser system appears to be limited. While not local, in the sense, of being a locally owned and -operated hospital with independent physicians, it appears to provide quite high-quality, reasonably priced services.

all of these acquisitions is to develop monopoly-like positions in various specialties, decrease costs as low as possible, and wherever the government extends medical coverage to that area, as this ensures a market with a payer that makes possible price increases.

The takeover of the kidney dialysis market is an excellent example of how PE operates in the healthcare field by identifying a hospital function, creating a freestanding practice, and then undercutting the hospital's (pricing by lowering quality and service) operation, thereby attracting insurance and Medicare patients. This forces the hospital to cease its operations. With this accomplished, the PE-backed operation can raise prices. This process has been repeated in healthcare function after function. Rather than list here all the functions PE has penetrated, we refer readers to Laura Katz Olson's (2022) book, *Ethically Challenged,* which is a comprehensive study of how PE penetrates various healthcare functions. In many respects, the transformation that happened in the emergency room has been repeated in other fields. In this section, drawing upon Olson (2022), we briefly review PE penetration and transformation of kidney dialysis as an example.

Kidney dialysis went from an in-hospital procedure to one practiced in freestanding clinics. In 1972, given the rising cases of diabetes, Congress extended coverage to those suffering from renal failure to all citizens. This immediately created a large and what would prove to be a growing market as obesity and diabetes caused greater renal failure. In 2022, Olson (2022, p. 111) reported that it had grown to a $34.7 billion industry and was continuing to grow rapidly as the need increased and the industry was able to push up prices. The four largest dialysis chains have been or are currently owned by PE firms. Given the drive to increase profitability, it is not surprising that facilities owned by PE investors have significantly higher mortality rates than hospitals (Olson, 2022, p. 114). Kidney dialysis has been transformed into a powerful profit center by Medicare reimbursement, but is largely unregulated, providing an incredible opportunity for profits.

Given the dilapidated and exploitative operation of these dialysis centers and the relative inaction of lawmakers to whom dialysis and PE firms make significant campaign contributions, the conditions are unsurprising. However, there have been various state attempts to regulate the activities of kidney dialysis centers. In California, where PE-owned dialysis firms made $3 billion in profits in 2018. In 2018, Proposition 8 proposed to cap profits and create minimum staffing standards for these largely unregulated clinics. The PE-owned dialysis clinics spent over $100 million to successfully defeat the proposition (Olson, 2022, p.115). In 2022, there was yet another proposition placed on the ballot to create minimum standards for dialysis clinics. And yet again, massive spending on heart-rending television advertisements by the PE-owned clinics defeated the proposition. The result is, of course, massive profits and healthcare outcomes that are far worse than other nations, but also worse than outcomes at nonprofit hospitals. Here again, PE firms used government regulations to unbundle what was formerly a part of the general hospital using the same playbook. First, the PE-owned clinics offer the service at a low cost – but with measurably lower quality (Olson, 2022, pp. 11–115). This pricing undercuts the hospital. In response, the hospital abandons the service because it is uncompetitive. Now that the superior competition has been vanquished, prices increase to whatever the market will bear. Unfortunately, as Eliason et al. (2022) found patients of dialysis clinics experience increases in mortality and hospitalization following acquisitions by a large corporate chain. The dialysis clinic is now extremely profitable at the cost of price, quality, and service. For the community, the general hospital now offers one less service, and the health of the community is reduced.

Dialysis centers are only one of many healthcare activities and hospital departments that have been penetrated by PE firms seeking to extract value from healthcare. We used dialysis as an example of the far broader phenomenon. The proliferation of these various healthcare facilities may appear as though they contribute to local economies, but their purpose is to extract value, leading to inferior healthcare, while weakening the local not-for-profit general hospitals. Given the deep penetration of PE into healthcare it is little wonder that the US spends a far greater percent of its GDP on healthcare than other developed nations while having worse outcomes. For local communities, this has meant the closure of hospitals in smaller communities, robbing them of healthcare options and making patients travel further for care.

PE has a larger influence as its entrance into an industry also creates a new sector logic. For example, when PE acquires a local dental office, it implements its toolkit – cutting costs and upselling. Due to economies of scale, the PE-owned dental office can offer services at a lower cost than the existing office, but the PE firm can offer incentives for upselling patients and share the return with the dentist. The dentist-employee could conceivably be better compensated than the dentist-owner, thereby incentivizing the dentist-owner to begin upselling their customers or selling their practice to a PE firm. The ultimate outcome is that a new short-term financial logic would take hold overthrowing the older professional code in medical care.

Ambulances

When we dial 911 for an ambulance for an emergency, the chances are that PE will respond. Patients have no control over which ambulance comes in response to their emergency, which creates an opportunity for price-gouging (United States Government Accountability Office, 2019). Two PE firms, American Securities and KKR, control almost two-thirds of the national market for air ambulances (Chhabra et al., 2020). Ground ambulances transport about 3 million privately insured patients to emergency rooms each year, with private companies providing one-thirds of those rides. While consumers expect insurance to cover the costs of transport after an accident, most patients receive a surprise bill, with a median bill amount of almost $22,000 for air transport and a median bill of $450 for ground transport. Congress last year enacted the *No Surprises Act*, which prohibits unexpected out-of-network bills, however, the protections do not apply to ground ambulance services. Many localities that once ran their own, nonprofit ambulance teams are now serviced by one of a few massive corporations, with frequent service disruption as assets are traded with little regard for the community. In 2016, PE owned twelve ambulance companies with three filed for bankruptcy from 2013–2016 (Ivory et al., 2016a).

Veterinary Services and Pet Supplies

PE firms also extract value from our pets. From 2017 to 2022, PE investment in the veterinary sector totaled over $45 billion (Prete, 2022). In 2015, the PE firm, BC Partners, purchased PetSmart and implemented the PE strategy. Not long afterwards, reports of animals dying due to understaffing and other forms of neglect were reported (Ballou, 2023b). In contrast the human healthcare, veterinary clinics are cash-based businesses. Remarkably, veterinary prices increased faster than human medical services (Ballou, 2023b).

Vets were traditionally highly trusted professionals but with consolidation and PE financing, the familiar story of increased prices and declining quality is reported (Carroll, 2023). Of course, veterinary services are only a small part of a local community, but veterinary services and vets are another segment of independent professional businesses, often women-owned, that was another piece in the jigsaw of a resilient independent community that has been replaced by an algorithm-driven extractive logic built upon upselling to grief-stricken pet owners. In the next section, we turn to another vital sector of any community – housing.

Housing

Housing is an enormous asset class encompassing multi-family, single-family, and mobile home residences. In 2023, US residential real estate was estimated to be worth $43 trillion (Malone, 2023) and in 2021 multifamily dwellings were worth another $3.8 billion (Nareit, 2021). Yet housing is more than an investment – it is an essential item for individual, family, and community quality of life. Housing proved to be a perfect industry for PE investors, as demand is inelastic – that is to say, the families and households will pay whatever the market demands to avoid the alternative of becoming homeless and living on the streets. PE competes against families to buy the limited supply of housing. With PE owning the home, instead of building wealth for residents, these homes are now a vehicle for profits, with rents increasing while quality and maintenance decline. PE's entrance into housing, like so many other sectors, was facilitated by government policy.

PE has become a powerful actor in housing markets beginning in the 2000s. During the Housing Bubble in 2005, PE firms bought 100,000 units of rent-stabilized housing in New York City. These properties were formerly not considered good investments because of a rent control policy that kept the units' monthly rental fees below that of similar apartments. But due to deregulation, that calculation changed. PE firms bought up entire buildings to convert these properties to market prices, using bank loans to pay wildly over-inflated prices. To pay back these loans, the investors had to either drive the affordable rent-protected tenants out and/or decrease maintenance, both of which they proceeded to do. To encourage tenants to leave the new owners harassed tenants "by filing building-wide eviction notices, baseless lawsuits for unpaid rent, aggressive buy-out offers, refusal to make repairs inside units, and threats to call immigration authorities." As a result, tenant advocates termed the new owners as "predatory equity" (Fields, 2015, pp. 149–150). After the 2008 Financial Crisis, various tenants' rights groups were able to pressure local governments for some relief especially as a number of these early PE investors were foreclosed by the banks.

As memorialized in the movie "The Big Short," mortgages became vehicles for unbridled financial speculation. The 2008 mortgage ravaged entire communities as millions of homeowners defaulted on predatory loans. Ellen and Dastrup (2012) estimated that $7 trillion in home equity evaporated during the crisis with many losing everything. However, the Obama Administration rather than rein in financialization and support the homeowners decided that PE could be part of the "solution."[12] After the federal government bailed out the Federal National Home Association (FMHA) and its sister organization, Federal Home Loan Mortgage Corporation (FHLMC), these two organizations bought foreclosed loans from the private banks and then sold the homes to PE firms as bulk transactions as they were supposed to be easier to manage. This

---

[12] It was politically expedient for the Obama Administration officials to dispose of the mess by selling in bulk to private equity investors and not deal with "bailing out" homeowners from their "unwise" investments.

proved to be a massive wealth transfer to the PE buyers and whetted their appetite for residential real estate (Ballou, 2023a, Chapter 2; Fields, 2018).

These decisions by the Obama Administration attracted PE firms to purchase single-family residences (SFRs) and convert them into rental units as the housing market collapsed. Unsurprisingly, PE worked to cut operating costs to increase income. One of the solutions was to manage these properties through online platforms (Fields, 2022), removing on-site property managers, to provide service to tenants such as handling routine maintenance issues but also overseeing safety and routine functions. There is evidence that PE firms have slighted maintenance, piled on unexpected fees and charges, and ignored their tenant's complaints (Ballou, 2023a, Chapter 2). In yet another ploy to extract more capital from its portfolio of SFRs, Blackstone-owned Invitation Homes was able to secure a government guarantee for its securitization of future rent payments. This allowed for the sale of securities that generated a dividend – a remarkable achievement – that made its investments even more profitable, with the government and taxpayers accepting all the risk (Richter, 2017). Moreover, with government rent payment guarantees, Blackstone and other PE firms qualify to pay a lower interest rate, thereby favoring it over individual buyers who wish to take out a mortgage to buy a home (for further information see Table 4). Unsurprisingly, PE investors have plunged into SFR purchases: PE is estimated to own approximately 5 percent of all SFRs in the United States,

Table 4 Private equity-owned and -backed single-family rental companies, June 2022.

Private Equity Firm	Rental Company	Single-Family Homes Controlled
Pretium Partners / Ares Management	Progress Residential	80,000
Blackstone	Tricon American Homes ($300 M stake)	31,032
	Home Partners of America	23,724
Cerberus Capital	FirstKey Homes	35,899
Amherst Securities/ Stone Point Capital	Amherst Residential	33,219
Access Capital	Vinebrook Homes	21,144
Brookfield Asset Management	Conrex Property Management (Connorex-Lucinda)	10,000

Americans for Financial Reform (2022).

with an estimate that this could grow to 40 percent by 2030 (Baker, 2022). PE portfolio firms (some of which have made public offerings) own even larger concentrations of SFRs in markets such as Atlanta, Phoenix, and Tampa (Colburn et al., 2021; Miller, 2022).

PE firms have become important buyers of new housing, accounting for 18 percent of single-family home sales nationally (Sherman, 2022). Eason (2023) reported that families were outbid by investors for a home only to then have to rent from those same investors, who disproportionately target starter homes in communities of color. Rather than a local owner, the new model is the remote digital landlord, with all aspects of the relationship managed online, making it difficult to get service, resolve disputes, and simultaneously eliminate local jobs. Rather than regarding housing as an essential need and an important locus of family and individual life, real estate simply became another asset class.

During the last thirty years, real estate has become increasingly financialized as apartment buildings and mobile home parks went from being individually and locally owned to being owned by large national and global investors. PE investors have also been extremely active in purchasing apartment buildings, owning approximately 1 million apartment units in the United States or 3.6 percent of all apartments in the country. Importantly, a significant percentage of these were made with the support of the Federal government's FHLMC (Federal Home Loan Mortgage Corporation or Freddie Mac). While only a small portion of all the total loans were financed by the federal agency, the PE firms accounted for 85 percent of FHLMC's twenty largest deals to finance apartment complex purchases. The largest of these was for nearly $1.8 billion (Vogell, 2022b)

Mobile home parks have attracted significant attention from PE. This sector often ignored is significant as a housing choice with approximately twenty million US citizens living in mobile homes (also known as manufactured housing). Mobile-home parks are the largest sources of nonsubsidized, low-income housing in the country very often serving senior citizens, veterans, and people with disabilities (Sullivan, 2018). Residents often buy their manufactured homes that often are not really mobile, thus their investment is actually fixed spatially. Normally, they rent the land that their homes occupy and, because the homes are expensive to move, they are very vulnerable to rent increases – a fact that PE firms recognize and thus, after acquiring the mobile home park dramatically increase the rent – confident that the residents will not move. Further, mobile home dwellers are excluded from the basic legal protections that cover tenants in rented houses or apartments, such as mandatory notice periods for rent increases and evictions (Kolhatkar, 2021). The captured nature of mobile homeowners makes investment attractive to PE firms. Finally, if the land is sufficiently valuable it can developed for another purpose driving the renters out completely.

University dorm housing, with its captured clientele, has also attracted PE firms (Light, 2022). In 2022, for the first time, the average rents for purpose-built student housing grew faster (8.8 percent) than did rents for regular multi-family housing (Alonso, 2023). To illustrate, in 2022 PE giant, Blackstone acquired American Campus Communities, which owned 166 properties located on or around 71 large university campuses for $13 billion. This was added to the more than $7 billion worth of student housing it already owned. To complete the circle, Blackstone received a multibillion-dollar bailout from the University of California's Board of Regents (Gallagher, 2023). Remarkably, student housing, which used to be owned and operated by universities, has been sold to PE firms.

Advances in technology have been the linchpin in the corporate consolidation of housing. Without innovations like cloud and mobile computing, digital plat-form architectures and business models, and massive data sets and the algorithms that sort them, it would not have been possible for large investors to take advantage of the market dislocation caused by the 2008 crisis (Fields & Vergerio, 2022). These new information technologies enabled firms like Invitation Homes (backed by Blackstone until 2019) to monitor markets at scale, rapidly evaluate and submit offers on homes that meet their investment criteria, and "efficiently" manage large, geographically dispersed portfolios of single-family rental homes. Corporate landlords have built powerful in-house data platforms fueled by algorithms that rapidly evaluate and submit offers on homes meeting investment criteria. With their vertically integrated corporate structures, institutional-scale landlords have access to a continuous flow of data about tenants and operating costs, which allows them to seek operating efficien-cies and new market opportunities. Unparalleled access to precision technologies, data, and digital analytics underpins the institutionalization of single-family residents (Fields & Vergerio, 2022, p. 12).

This is a story of inelastic demand with little bargaining power providing a reliable source of income that can be managed digitally with little account-ability guaranteeing a high rate of return. In 2022, there was an antitrust lawsuit filed in Texas that alleges that these giant PE housing owners share their data with a software firm, RealPage, that is also owned by PE firms. RealPage is then used by firms to algorithmically "collude" in setting rental prices (Vogell, 2022b). In the process, local citizens experience higher rents and degraded quality of service, while smaller, local landlords who may know and care about their tenants are squeezed out of the market. When citizens try to use the ballot to curb the abuses of these nonlocal PE landlords, the PE firms pour money into stopping the ballot initiatives and invest in ensuring that politicians favorable to their interests are elected. And, if on the off chance local regulations meant to control their activities pass, the PE firms invest in high-powered legal firms to take the local government to courts that have been packed by neoliberal judges. Finally, PE uses state and federal preemption to impose zoning and building code restrictions to override local discretion, as a final resort. Local laws and jurisdictions are anathema to PE firms and their supporters, as they form barriers to the unfettered flow and prerogatives of capital.

Supermarkets

Supermarkets are core institutions for any community and their closure can result in food "deserts" that have dire health and well-being impacts on the surrounding community whether urban or rural. Since the early 2000s, PE firms have invested repeatedly in supermarket chains consolidating operations (see Table 5). Supermarket chains are attractive to PE investors for a number of reasons: First and foremost, rollups could result in oligopolistic concentration whereby customers had fewer choices allowing the supermarket to increase prices (Tkacik, 2022). Increased size creates greater leverage for bargaining with suppliers; many of whom have also been consolidating – often under the tutelage of their PE owners. Often, the land and facilities could be liquified by selling and leasing them back, thereby releasing significant amounts of capital that were used to pay "special dividends" to the PE owners.

As in all of our cases, workers are one of the first victims. In the 1940s and 1950s, supermarket chains unionized and the workers were paid significantly more than the nonunionized workers that staffed most retail stores. These unionized workers not only had higher pay and benefits, but for many supermarket chains their pensions were significant liabilities decreasing the overall "value" of the firm – if these could be discharged the value of the firm would increase (Batt & Appelbaum, 2018). These conditions thus were significant opportunities for PE investors to increase the value of their investment.

As with PE acquisitions in other industries, supermarket takeover strategies such as "prepackaged" bankruptcies to shed pension fund liabilities have been used (Appelbaum & Batt, 2018, p. 4). Through their various roll-ups, bankruptcies, and store closures, 10,000s of workers have lost their jobs, even as food deserts across the US have expanded (Hamidi, 2020). PE-owned firms are very focused on the financial returns of individual stores and, unsurprisingly, in their efforts to improve profitability, and stores located in small towns and poorer neighborhoods were abandoned.

Supermarkets are critical institutions in local communities. PE investors, as can be seen from Table 5, have bought chains resulting in the closure of more

Table 5 Supermarket chains acquired by private equity, rolled up competitors, headquarters location, number of employees, date of acquisition, and status

Supermarket Chain	Rolled Up Competitors	Headquarters (if known)	PE Firms	Number of Employees	Status, Date of Bankruptcy	Date of Acquisition (if known)
A&P	Food Basics, Food Emporium, Pathmark, Super Fresh, Waldbaum's	New York City	Yucaipa	28,500	2015	2009
Fairway Market	None	New York City	Sterling	4,000	2016	2007
Fresh & Easy	None	El Segundo, CA	Yucaipa	4,000	2015	2013
Marsh	None	Indianapolis, IN	Sun	14,000	2017	2006
Southeastern Grocers	Bi-Lo, Bruno's, Fresco y Mas, Harveys, Winn-Dixie[a]	Jacksonville, FL	Lone Star	50,000	2009, 2018	2005
Tops Markets	Grand Union	Buffalo, NY	Morgan Stanley	14,800	2018	2007

Albertsons	Safeway, Lucky, Vons, Jewel-Osco, Haggen, Acme[a]	Boise, ID	Cerberus	270,000	Operating	2006
Save Mart	Save Mart, Lucky, Lucky California, Food Maxx, and Maxx Value Foods	Modesto, CA	Kingswood	14,000	Operating	2022
Ralphs	ABC Markets, Alpha Beta, Boys Markets, and Cala Foods	Los Angeles, CA	Yucaipa	28,000	1997 Sold to Kroger	1994

[a] Complex series of acquisitions, spin-offs, and recapitalizations.
Adapted and extended from Batt and Appelbaum (2018).

than 1,500 stores due to bankruptcy alone (Batt & Appelbaum, 2018) with hundreds more closed in cost-cutting exercises. Communities were impoverished as unions were weakened and even, more directly, when the PE owners reneged on the firm's pension obligations. Moreover, the roll-ups meant that control of these supermarkets, which previously had been regional, was increasingly distant and thus less amenable to local influence. In the process, supermarket workers, food consumers, and the local tax base have been harmed by the extractive activities of the PE industry.

Newspapers

"In America, there is scarcely a hamlet which has not its own newspaper."
—Alexis De Tocqueville (1835: Chapter 9)

PE played a significant role in the demise of local newspapers and a corresponding lack of reporting on local events and providing civic information important to communities. Newspapers played an important role in democracy and local opinion formation. When observing the US and the factors that supported the early American democratic experiment, De Tocqueville noted, "Nothing is easier than to set up a newspaper, and a small number of readers suffices to defray the expenses of the editor" continuing "the number of periodical and occasional publications which appears in the United States actually surpasses belief." At the time, these newspapers were often crude but served as a source of public order and local control of politics important to democracy Local newspapers provide information about local concerns, provide transparency for public meetings, and report on civic and social events. Since 2005, roughly 2,200 local newspapers have closed, as the number of newspapers per hundred million population fell from 1,200 (in 1945) to 400 in 2014. The number of newspaper journalists has decreased from 43,000 in 1978 to 33,000 in 2015 (Kamarck & Gabrielle, 2015). The consolidation of US media has been an ongoing process. As these newspapers closed or were amalgamated, the news became ever more standardized. PE and other investment partnerships moved quickly to acquire hundreds of distressed newspapers and in 2023 they owned seven of the largest twenty-five newspapers.

The conventional, and overly simple explanation, is that the internet killed the news. Yet, advertising revenue for newspapers peaked in 2006 at $50 billion. This was more than ten years after the Internet became a commercial medium. Certainly, the internet had a role in the decline of news publishing. However, the entry of PE as it acquired not only local newspapers but also television and radio stations contributed to increased industry concentration. PE firms, following the pattern of buying distressed businesses, increased their share of America's newspaper industry from around 5 percent in 2002 to 23 percent in 2019 (Pew). PE firms cut reporting staff and reduced local coverage more than other types of owners (Ewens et al., 2022). PE owners cut back local news coverage, ran more national news content, and decreased the number of articles by nearly 20 percent.

When studying PE buyouts of local newspapers, Ewens et al. (2022) found that following PE buyouts, in elections of county commissions and councils, mayoral and sheriff elections both total votes and turnout declined. Further, the fraction of people with no opinion about their U.S. House Representative increased by two percentage points (relative to a mean of 18 percent), but had no effect on opinions about the U.S. President. These results suggest lower participation in local democracy after PE buyouts, almost certainly driven by the decline in local news coverage that was instituted as a cost-savings measure.

Payday Loans

This lack of access to banking and the lack of individual ability to secure loans has given rise to the payday loan industry. Payday loans are short-term loans for less than $10,000, with high-interest rates. While pawn shops have long existed, payday lending exploded in the late nineties (Stegman, 2007). Due to extensive industry lobbying[13], payday lenders are highly profitable and unregulated. Annual percentage rates (APR) can range above 600 percent when add-on insurance and service fees are included. In 2021, there were approximately 23,000 payday lenders in the United States, of which at least 5,000 are owned by PE firms.

Payday lenders serve a unique function as the household lender of last resort. Morse (2011) demonstrates that following natural disasters, the presence of payday lenders reduces foreclosures and larcenies. Melzer (2011) finds access to payday loans decreases households' ability to pay mortgage, rent, and utility bills. Driven by need, with limited options payday lending offers a means to prey on the most vulnerable in society and creates a cycle of debt traps that threaten the most vulnerable (Whoriskey, 2018). Predatory practices have been exposed in lawsuits. A 2022 lawsuit against the PE firm, Mariner which has 480 branches in 22 states notes, "Mariners's policies and procedures are set and directed by headquarters, leaving minimal discretion to branch managers and loan officers to extend loans that work best for consumers according to their need and financial conditions" (Case 2:22-CV-03253). In another case, Elevate Credit paid $33 million to resolve litigation with Tribal Nations (Pierre-Louis, 2023). As always, it was the enormous profitability of this industry has induced PE to invest and increase the footprint of this most predatory of financial institutions.

---

[13] For details on political contributions and lobbying, see paydaylendingfacts.org.

Cradle to Grave

The provision of childcare services has been fragmented, with many providers, serving geographically distinct markets. The industry has been consolidating, with large national chains, including familiar names like KinderCare Learning Centers (Partners Group), Bright Horizons (Bain Capital with IPO in 2013), Primrose School (Roark Capital), and Goddard Systems (Sycamore Partners). Indeed, nine of the top eleven for-profit childcare providers, including all the top five, are backed by PE (Haspel, 2023). Collectively, these investor-backed chains serve over 750,000 young children every day, representing a roughly 10 percent market share within childcare. Consolidation occurred to realize economies of scale. PE funds have been consolidating by buying up services. While the typical community-based center operates with thin profit margins, the chain centers can expect annual profits of 15 percent to 20 percent of revenue (Goldstein, 2022). PE firms lobbied against Biden's Build Back Better legislation, which would have created a near-universal childcare system and limiting childcare payments to 7 percent of family income for all but the wealthiest families (Goldstein, 2022). This US decision occurred roughly in parallel with Canada instituting a universal $10-a-day childcare program (Yong, 2023).

PE firms are also investing in behavioral services for children and adolescents, including services for youth with intellectual and developmental disabilities, services for youth in foster care, services for youth in the juvenile justice system, troubled teen programs, and autism services (O'Grady, 2022). These care services are contracted out by state and local governments and are largely unregulated.

The PE entry into nursing homes, skilled care, and other such facilities has been nothing short of breath-taking and tragic – and really questions the US's willingness to care for our older population. Here again, the logic of wealth extraction is absolutely dominant and transformative. Unsurprisingly, Gupta et al. (2021) find that PE acquisitions of nursing homes increase short-term mortality and decrease the reported well-being of patients – in a familiar refrain they find that the acquisitions were financed by borrowing that puts pressure on the facility in terms of cost.[14]

For the last act, PE has aggressively entered the funeral home industry. Typically, funeral homes are a venerable and high-touch local service. In many towns, the funeral home is a stately building, prominently located and run by the same family for generations. PE is attracted to this industry by

---

[14] For further confirmation see also Braun et al. (2021). For a microlevel understanding of the changes PE brings to a nursing home, see Rafiel (2022).

high-profit margins, the inevitability of death, and the ability to cut costs by leveraging economies of scale in purchasing, administration, and marketing. Despite these arguments for cost savings, prices increase. For example, Angel Valley Funeral Home in Tucson Arizona was sold to PE-backed Foundation Partners Group in 2019, with prices increasing from $425 to $760 for a cremation, from $1,840 to $2,485 for a burial with no viewing or visitation, and from $3,405 to $4,480 for a full, economical funeral (Hawryluk, 2022). For private funeral home operators, their reputation is their strongest asset, limiting opportunistic behavior at an emotionally vulnerable time.

Education

While K-12 education to date has received little investment from PE firms, other parts of the educational system have attracted PE investment. Another pernicious area of PE investment is for-profit technical schools and universities. These for-profit educational organizations have a long history of abusing their customers, a.k.a. students. Eaton et al. (2020) found that PE buyouts lead to higher tuition and per-student debt. As has been seen in every sector, PE-owned schools capture government aid and after the buyouts spent less, had lower graduation rates, higher loan repayment rates, and lower earnings among graduates.

These abuses have been exposed in Congressional hearings and investigative reporting but little has been done to halt their activities (Eaton et al., 2020). A 2017 study showed that for-profit schools received nearly 90 percent of their income from federal student assistance programs (Kelchen, 2017). Until recently, the US Department of Defense allowed for-profit universities to recruit students on military bases, all of whom had veteran's educational benefits (Burke, 2023). Only in 2023 did Congress propose laws providing the veterans with the ability to sue these firms for failure to deliver promised services.

PE firms investing in education deploy the same playbook as they do in other fields. What is remarkable is the educational benefits that our government provides to citizens and, in particular, veterans are hijacked by PE firms, that often have investments from universities such as Harvard, Stanford, and the University of California endowments, and little or no real education is delivered. But, more importantly, the dreams and ambitions of these young people are stolen, and, in many respects, the public benefits are squandered. The net loss to society is incalculable. For communities, for-profit university students siphon off from community colleges. In contrast, these for-profit universities have a very small local footprint and pay their employees and instructors poorly.

Home Repair

The universe of PE investor targets appears to be constantly expanding with greater destruction of local ownership. In 2023, an article in *Bloomberg News* entitled "Why Private Equity Is Chasing Plumbers and Lumber Yards" was published (Sasso, 2023). This article captured the increased interest of PE in smaller private local service firms that have developed a local or regional market niche. A recent example from June 2021, was the consolidation by the PE firm, Grove Mountain Partners, of twelve East Coast HVAC firms (Mesenbrink, 2023). These local recession-resistant industries, in some ways, resemble healthcare in that demand for these services is inelastic as repairs are not discretionary when problems arise. Of course, if homeowners cannot afford the repairs they might live without air conditioning or not repair the plumbing thereby allowing the housing stock to deteriorate as it has in many cities. Earlier, a typical market would have a large number of small providers with competition keeping prices under control. However, the massive entry into these industries has, as Tim Clarke, PitchBook's lead PE analyst, was quoted, "If you acquire enough, you get economies of scale . . . You just keep rolling rolling, rolling and before you know it you've got 10–20 percent of the market (Sasso, 2023)." What Clarke did not mention is that when two or three PE firms can capture 30, 40, 50, or 60 percent of the market, oligopolistic collusion can occur simply through price signaling. In these local markets, there is no scrutiny by any regulators either at the time of acquisition or afterward.

Similar tactics used elsewhere, such as cost-saving from buying parts in volume, using lower quality parts, decreasing wages for experienced technicians, hiring unqualified personnel, increasing prices to whatever the market will bear, and extensive advertising allow PE back companies to achieve powerful local market share. Once again, developing large local market share can turbocharge profitability and thus increase the value of the now rolled-up set of firms for a corporate buyer. For home services, there is far less government regulation, political concern, or press scrutiny.

Municipal Infrastructure and Public Goods

PE firms are actively working to access the $2.9 trillion that state and local governments spent in 2019 (Nunn et al., 2019). PE investors have been delighted to create "public-private partnerships" where they acquire and manage public infrastructure. Investments are often hailed as partnerships but rather are privatizations where cash-strapped cities sell their service operations to the private sector. This is part of the neoliberal agency that favors fiscal austerity and greater dependence on the market and the private sector. Invariably the long-run costs to taxpayers and citizens are greater than public ownership. As importantly, the public loss key public assets diminishes a municipalities' ability to pursue others and make investments. Invariably, with the PE extraction model the service levels decrease and the price for service in cases as the PE investors move to extract value from the asset as rapidly as possible. Finally, the value created by this infrastructure does not remain local but rather is transferred to the PE investors, thereby initiating a local divider effect that siphons off tax revenue.

There has been a long-standing philosophical debate about the balance between the public and private provision of government services. In the United States, this debate is noted to go back to the Revolutionary War with the procurement of armaments. When government provides services there has been a constant refrain that there will be waste, fraud, and abuse on the part of politicians and the, often unionized, public employees. These criteria have become dominant over concerns about equity, access, and the quality of service. Advocates of privatization promise greater efficiency and a reduction in the costs of service delivery, although the empirical evidence does not bear out the promise of lower costs and anecdotal evidence suggests that service quality declines, especially if PE is involved in the privatization (Mann & Warner, 2019).

Concurrent with the rise of neoliberalism, the sale of municipal services to PE began in the late 1970s. The ideology implicit in public choice theory and the new public management supported outsourcing public services in the putative name of greater efficiency. This ideology combined with the increasingly straitened local government budgets convinced local governments to begin privatizing municipal water and sanitation operations, solid waste disposal, parking revenues, and emergency and social services (Ivory et al., 2016b). This decision to move public assets to private ownership and/or control invariably results in the breaking of public-sector unions, whose members live locally, reducing any multiplier effects from their local spending.

Shrinking populations and a declining industrial base have led to chronic budget deficits for many small and medium-sized communities. In contrast to the federal government, state and local governments are required to balance their budgets. Their only remedy has been to engage in complex privatization schemes, selling off or monetizing their assets, including stadiums, parkland, and utilities. One of the most dramatic and widespread sales of former municipal services is the privatization of water systems, which provide a fundamental necessity (Grant, 2013).

Infrastructure is expensive to provide and requires constant maintenance. The water and sewer systems in the United States are over 100 years old. Consider Pittsburgh: The American Society of Civil Engineers estimated that a minimum investment of $39 billion between 2010 and 2030 would be required just to update Pittsburgh's water infrastructure with another $1.3 billion per year to treat the water supply (Zessoules, 2022). PE was very willing to join in. The city of Flint, Michigan offers another example of the lack of attention to this fundamental public service and the dangers of privatization. Both Pittsburgh and Flint ended their relationship with private entities in closed-door litigation.

Cash-strapped localities have privatized their water and sewer services. Often referred to as public-private partnerships these deals are found in any community that finds itself in financial difficulty. There are many different types of contractual arrangements covering operations, management, and ownership arrangements of water systems (National Research Council, 2002). Many municipalities lack the necessary technical expertise to negotiate complex water privatization contracts, providing a disadvantage in bargaining. This is exacerbated further by the fact that PE often bargains in bad faith or later decides to violate the terms and conditions forcing the community to sue in courts that are invariably packed with judges whose main goal is to uphold the rights of capital investment against the constraints of tradition, culture, and community.

Private acquisition of municipal utilities is a last resort source of capital. In the United States, government borrowing is the preferred funding mechanism.[15] Publicly owned utilities can issue tax-exempt municipal bonds that offer an advantage as bondholders do not have to pay federal income taxes on their earned interest. Yet, struggling municipalities have low credit ratings and are unable to competitively issue bonds. The sale of a municipal asset provides a one-shot infusion of capital.

One rationale for privatizing of water systems is the promise of efficiency gains and cost savings. Yet reviews of the evidence suggest that there is no significant difference in costs or efficiency between public and private production (Bel & Warner, 2008; Bel et al., 2010). One study that followed the ten largest known sales of municipal water or sewer systems to for-profit companies found that typical household water bills had nearly tripled since privatization,

---

[15] In fact, prior to World War Two local jurisdictions usually resorted to accumulating capital in a sinking fund and thus paying as they went.

increasing at an average of about three times the rate of inflation, and adding hundreds of dollars to annual household bills (Food & Water Watch, 2011). Water systems are essentially natural monopolies. They are capital-intensive and it is cost-prohibitive to have multiple providers serve the same location, resulting in a captive customer base. Public control of a natural monopoly can help ensure that service is widely available. A private firm in a monopoly position would act to maximize profits by raising prices and excluding service to those customers who are unable to pay. Municipalities that own their water utilities are more likely to have policies to protect low-income residents from disconnection. A greater risk is that once all the value has been taken out of the water system and it is close to collapse then the private firm will walk away leaving the residents without service. While the private sector benefits from short-term returns, the public sector is left responsible for long-term impacts (Merme et al., 2014,p. 20).

The higher prices of private services do not result in investment in the water system infrastructure – quite the opposite. For example, in 2011 the Missoula, Montana water system was sold to the Carlyle Group. The Carlyle Group extracted the maximum income from its investment by neglecting maintenance while raising prices before selling it to a Canadian firm (Douglass, 2017). During this period, the system degraded so badly that half of the water flowing through its pipes was lost. In June 2017, Missoula completed the condemnation process and paid $95 million including attorney fees to reacquire the system – after the assets had been run down, rates raised, and service quality lowered (Weiser, 2017).[16]

In the neoliberal era, politicians and others have urged local communities to privatize infrastructure and public utilities because, allegedly, private management will improve efficiency, presumably driving costs down. Nearly always, in these situations, the PE investors are far better bargainers than the local governments and make commitments that are very difficult to enforce after the transaction has closed.

Where to go from here?

This section has demonstrated the remarkable growth in the scope of PE investing during the last four decades, touching every sector of the economy. This investment, rather than increasing capacity, depletes the existing assets of the businesses acquired in an effort to maximize profit. While financial services

---

[16] Further complex litigation between Carlyle and the City of Missoula that might require the City to pay Carlyle even more money, as the Carlyle Group exacts its final pound of flesh through the legal system (Szpaller, 2021).

are essential to any economy, the PE model reduces the resources that provide resilience and adaptability to change. For communities, this has meant a deterioration in quality even as prices for goods and services increase, thereby extracting increasing amounts of value out of our communities. In many cases, so much value is extracted that the operation is closed, thereby depriving the community of that service. Effectively, many communities lose the diversity of services that provide it with resilience and cohesion. Small local businesses are replaced by national chains or rolled up into larger entities managed to extract the maximum amount of profit. Going back to the multiplier concept, there are fewer and fewer local businesses that keep profits local and as a result, communities suffer.

PE is part of a larger system of financialization that has become dominant over the past forty years. These changes occurred as the quality and length of life for the average US resident has decreased by any number of measures and income inequality has increased, both among different groups of citizens but also geographically. Of course, PE is only accountable to the narrowest definition of profitability. All other dimensions of life and society are assumed away in the name of profitability. Investors, believing in their claims of higher-than-average rates of return are happy to look away. This entire system is structured and incentivized to operate against community and social welfare.

It is difficult to imagine what sectors PE may target next, although, while preparing this Element, we were surprised to learn the full range of activities where PE already operates. Without intervention, PE will continue to seek out other sectors and activities from which to extract value. After earning large returns by going into new sectors and wringing market efficiencies, the easy and affordable targets may be limited and the pursuit of return may become desperate and predatory. Consider the ownership and management of prisons, following the healthcare model of divesting activities to subsidiaries which then charge inmates for healthcare, personal products, and phone calls – a literal captive market. Without regulation, PE will also increase its market power in existing sectors by expanding its market share and becoming local monopolies.

The next section explores policies to reverse the hold that PE has on communities and our society. It took forty years to reach the current situation but it does not have to take forty years to reverse the damage. All that is needed is to restore local autonomy, discourage business roll-ups, regulate extractive investment, and invest in productive activities. Going back to the multiplier concept, there are fewer and fewer local businesses that keep profits local and communities suffer.

4 What Kind of Future Do We Want?

> Knowledge is power: You hear it all the time but knowledge is not power. It's only potential power. It only becomes power when we apply it and use it. Somebody who reads a book and doesn't apply it, they're at no advantage over someone who's illiterate.
>
> None of it works unless YOU work. We have to do our part. If knowing is half the battle, action is the second half of the battle."
>
> — Jim Kwik (n.d.)

Writing and reading this Element would be unbearable if we could not end with a few constructive solutions. Most simply, reducing the negative impact of PE requires addressing the conditions that make PE profitable in the first place. Our original intention was to more generally examine the reasons for the demise of local economies. But everywhere we looked PE was making investments and transforming our society. So, we decided to focus on PE, with its emphasis on value extraction rather than new productive investment, a root cause for the demise of local economies

The Neoliberal transformation of capitalism has failed the average American. Even for those doing well economically, it is hard to ignore the crisis of homelessness, the deaths of despair, and a medical system that is over-priced, unavailable to many and delivers low quality to most citizens. Our economic experiment with the doctrine *Greed is Good* has run its course. The Neoliberal experiment unleashed a tsunami of debt-leveraged acquisitions that have destroyed entire sectors of our economy – a process aided and abetted by government policy. The result has been an economy that cannot provide personal protective equipment in respond to a health crisis, is indifferent to the climate crisis, and provides ever lower quality products and services. Economic power has become increasingly concentrated in nearly all industries, and, most worrisome, our wealth is increasingly ill-distributed.

It does not have to be this way. The nature of the corporation and the type of finance available is the product of political resolve and accountability.[17] Just as the Progressive Era was a response to the corruption, monopoly power, and inequality of the Robber Barron Era that brought about the Gilded Age and the New Deal followed the Great Depression, our era requires an adjustment aimed at addressing and even banishing the abuses that PE exemplifies. The United States currently practices a specific variety of capitalism that favors financialization and incentivizes the operation of PE. This contrasts with the varieties of capitalism

---

[17] Oreskes and Convey (2023) document how American business organizations engaged in a campaign to promote neoliberalism, teaching Americans that the government could not be trusted and did not have their interests at heart – and in the current configuration there is ample evidence that this is the case.

practiced in Northern Europe (Hall & Thelen, 2009). For example, the German variety of capitalism is governed by social institutions that guarantee high wages for a significant segment of the workforce while maintaining international competitive industries. The Nordic model, followed in Sweden, Norway, Finland, Denmark, and Iceland, merges free-market capitalism with a generous welfare system. Among these capitalist models, the United States has the highest levels of income inequality, with pronounced regional disparities.

This Element, with its focus on the impact of PE on local economies, is part of a series on Redefining Capitalism. While we are part of a global economy, we are physical beings – our homes, relationships, and communities define what it means to be human. Innovation and industrial productivity are the cornerstones of an economy and the locus of this activity is decidedly community-based. This is the logic of industrial clustering has been prominent beginning with early American industrial history. Local economies specialized in different industries, with firms learning from others close to them, integrating ideas from a specialized and dedicated labor force, and benefiting from suppliers who made creative suggestions. These are the conditions that Alfred Marshal noted when he wrote that, "the secrets of the industry are in the air" And the reasons that automotive manufacturing was concentrated in Detroit, pharmaceuticals in New Jersey, medical devices in Milwaukee, recreational vehicles in Elkhart Indiana, and glass production in Lancaster Ohio – the list goes on. Part of the advantage was state and local policies that created conditions that allowed local industry to flourish.

The Biden Administration has launched national policy initiatives to foster investments to reinvigorate local economies. However, constructive solutions meant to rebuild local capacity will not have their full impact, if we do not recognize that these initiatives are embedded in a system organized to incentivize the financialization of local economic assets. The short-term orientation of PE is the opposite of the type of investment needed to invigorate communities.

Addressing the demise of the local will require a comprehensive approach that will require a rebalancing of government at the national, state, and local levels to mitigate the total reliance on unfettered free markets. This will require a new regulation aimed at protecting citizens and encouraging long-term investment that prioritizes local businesses, workers, consumers, residents, and jobs. Any policies limiting practices employed by PE, and the finance industry more broadly, will experience enormous resistance. But just as financialization was introduced and institutionalized over time, it must be similarly dismantled by an ongoing process prosecuted at all levels of government and executed with resolve. There is a need to restore state and local sovereignty by limited preemption policies that favor national business interests. Policies that will reverse the PE that have devastated local economies are within reach.

Federal Reforms[18]

Over the last four decades, the PE has diligently worked to pass laws, transform the tax code, weaken regulations of all types to favor its activities, and unfortunately ignore the law entirely or pay fines for transgressions that are inadequate to deter the same behavior in the future. These trends can be reversed and used to ensure that PE does not work against the interests of local businesses, workers, and communities. There is a need for tax and legislative reforms that will discourage the practices of PE and focus on long-term investments focused on helping companies to grow and public sector entities to make investments in infrastructure, thereby expanding economic opportunity for communities and workers. This means transforming the environment that encourages PE. The ways that this can be done include the elimination of the preferential treatment of carried interest and the write-off of debt associated with leveraged buyouts, and actively prosecuting the use of roll-ups to establish monopoly power in local markets. None of these actions alone will be sufficient – it will require all of these and many other actions to transform finance to be conducive to long-term investments in local communities.

There is a need to impose guidelines for what has been an unregulated and opaque activity. A frank debate is needed about how to increase the positive benefits PE creates while mitigating the costs to society and the local community – or even if it is possible for PE to create enough value to justify the damage it does. For example, Senator Warren has introduced the descriptively titled *Stop Wall Street Looting Act*. The bill is part of a series of efforts based upon the belief that it is possible to reform PE by holding them responsible for their actions and those of their portfolio firms.[19] Similar types of legislation have been introduced repeatedly but have yet to pass. The perceived need to increase transparency and oversight gained traction after the Global Financial Crisis. The Dodd-Frank Act subjected PE fund managers to slightly greater oversight from regulators yet restrictions have been revoked under pressure from PE firms (Toyou, 2018).[20] The Dodd-Frank Act might be a framework that could be strengthened to improve securities laws that allow investors to make more informed decisions.

---

[18] The federal government has many tools to affect the operation of PE actions and others have written about the need for federal actions, including tax reform, increased regulation and the need for judicial action (Appelbaum & Batt, 2014, Chapter 9; Ballou, 2023b; Christophers, 2023, Chapter 6; Morgenson & Rosner, 2023, Chapter 17).

[19] Full transcripts of 2021 Hearings can be found at www.govinfo.gov/content/pkg/CHRG-117shrg52184/pdf/CHRG-117shrg52184.pdf.

[20] Barney Frank would later work to ease financial regulations as he joined the revolving door (Bycowicz, 2023). Christopher Dodd of Connecticut was very close to the financial sector (Mayer & Beckel, 2009) and after leaving the Senate became a lobbyist.

The easiest and most obvious PE reform would be to eliminate the carried interest provision, which is a subsidy to the owners of PE firms (i.e., general partners) that increases their after-tax return on investment. This preferential tax treatment allows the general partners to treat their carried interest income as capital gains, despite the fact their return is not a return on capital investment, but rather a form of income for investing and monitoring the portfolio companies. The carried interest is the income source that contributes to the massive returns reaped by the general partners, thereby creating enormous wealth that contributes greatly to our economic inequality.

There have been repeated attempts to repeal the carried interest tax benefit. The Trump administration failed to cut this tax loophole even though it was a key campaign promise, with Gary Cohn citing at least twenty-five attempts to change carried interest (Kim, 2017). In August 2022, provisions to limit carried interest were eliminated from President Biden's *Build Back Better* legislation. This outcome regarding one of the most egregious subsidies to PE shows exactly how difficult it will be to reverse the entire ecosystem of laws, court decisions, interpretations, and regulations that have evolved to facilitate PE operations.

Congress has already moved to limit the ability of firms to write off interest payments used in leveraged buyouts as a business expense. The 2017 tax cut legislation capped the amount of interest that could be deducted to 30 percent of a firm's adjusted income. This legislation was meant to decrease the attractiveness of debt for leveraged buyouts. However, ultimately it did little to reduce the pace of PE operations – while it has not been analyzed carefully – it is likely that the PE firms found ways of working around the restriction. Reducing the threshold further or even eliminating it entirely would make the leveraged buyout model less attractive. Debt is a reasonable business expense, if the owners invested in capital equipment or worker training designed to increase productivity, rather than the use of debt issued by the target firm, in essence, purchase itself.

Housing affordability is a crucial aspect of societal equity. PE take-over of housing is limiting access to safe and affordable housing. One simple step would be to eliminate PE tax benefits for the ownership of single- and multi-family residences, trailer parks, and dormitories.

The Federal Trade Commission (FTC) has a role in regulating the PE practice of business rolling up. In September 2023, the FTC filed an antitrust suit against U.S. Anesthesia Partners, Inc. (USAP), the dominant provider of anesthesia services in Texas, and the firm Welsh, Carson, Anderson & Stowe, alleging a multi-year anticompetitive roll-up scheme to consolidate anesthesiology practices, and drove up the price of anesthesia services provided to Texas patients. Lina Kahn, Federal Trade Commission Chair, has said that the FTC will begin scrutinizing roll-up deals involving small companies that compete in local markets (Kahn, 2024).

Previously, the small size of individual acquisitions was below a self-imposed threshold for being reported to the FTC. Recognizing that the summed value of multiple acquisitions allowed firms to amass significant control over key services in local markets, with serious consequences for consumers, workers, businesses, and communities, this action signals a new awakening in the interpretation and enforcement of antitrust laws.

Moreover, the Securities and Exchange Commission (SEC) announced in August 2023 the adoption of new rules and rule amendments to enhance the regulation of private fund advisers and update the existing compliance rule that applies to all investment advisers (U.S. Securities and Exchange Commission, 2023). These are designed to protect private fund investors by increasing transparency, competition, and efficiency in the private funds market. The greater scrutiny by the SEC is meant to protect investors such as the hapless pension funds where their PE investments have negative returns.

Yet another very powerful initiative would be for the Department of Labor could initiate rule-making that would limit the ability of pension plans to invest in PE, not only because of the inherent risks, but also because their investments have a negative impact on the society and communities where workers live. Similarly, Medicare and Medicaid could tighten up regulation of the healthcare facilities that they reimburse for services. For example, Medicare and Medicaid could undertake more inspections and statistical analysis to determine whether PE-owned facilities provide inferior care – and if this is found to be the case – special taskforces could be formed to target PE-owned facilities for aggressive inspection. We have shown that Federal programs and their dollars drive much of PE investment in healthcare, in particular. Aggressive enforcement would ensure that the federal dollars are well-spent and, in the process, lower the returns to PE investing. Federal regulatory authorities across all sectors should be alert to the possibility that PE is entering their mandated area and be vigilant regarding its pressure on the firms it acquires to violate regulations or impose unforeseen social costs in their pursuit of a rapid return. The federal government's regulatory machinery, which extends into all sectors of the economy, could be an enormous shield to protect citizens and reduce the damage that unbridled financial engineering has on the economy. Further, it could encourage state and local governments to create new solutions to the problems created by PE in their communities.

Promoting Experiments in the Laboratories of Democracy

Action at the state and local level will be vital to enact change and act like *laboratories of democracy,* as the constitution was interpreted by Justice Brandeis. Unfortunately, decision-making has become centralized removing the ability of state and local governments to respond to the actions of PE. Hopkins (2019) documents the nationalization of state policy: state party platforms are more alike; residents are less likely to know their governors' names; and, money for political races increasingly comes from out-of-state donors. This trend goes against the doctrine of federalism and voter sovereignty and has only intensified recently. With state and local oversight, it would have been more difficult to roll up businesses, loot employee pension plans, extract capital from cities and states, and transfer the value to a very few money centers such as Greater New York City. In the name of creating a good business climate, finance capital has engineered a race to the bottom as state governments crippled or abandoned entirely their oversight responsibilities, offered a wide variety of relocation or retention incentives, and reduced corporate tax rates, all in an attempt to attract or retain economic activity. The general idea that a favorable business climate would generate more tax revenue has not been realized but has created a rigged game in which companies are able to have states and municipalities bid against one another. The tangible results for communities of PE investment are lower wages, reduced worker protections, reduced service quality, higher prices, weakened pension funds, and diminished social safety nets – even as value is transferred to PE firms.

Local and state governments are critical as they are closest to communities and witness the impacts of job losses, service degradation, and local monopolization more immediately. Even state efforts such as using the California initiative process to control PE-owned kidney dialysis resulted in an onslaught of $233 million lobbying effort that ultimately ended in defeat. State attorneys general can and have acted to hold PE firms accountable for the actions of their portfolio firms. For example, in the fall of 2021, a PE fund agreed to pay $25 million in a settlement with the Massachusetts attorney general that was upheld by the U.S. District Court (Office of Attorney General Maura Healey, 2021). Rather than acting in isolation, states and local jurisdictions can join together to initiate lawsuits to challenge the status quo.

There are many possibilities and opportunities for state and local jurisdictions to protect their communities and reverse the reach of PE. This begins by recognizing the number of limitations imposed by uniform cut-and-paste, one size fits all, legislation that limits responsiveness to the needs of residents, and limits democratic representation. For one, it has often left state governments with more to do and less functioning or fiscal capacity. States, in turn, passed on limitations to localities, which hamstrings efforts to provide needed services or initiatives that municipalities have enacted.

US federalism is predicated on the assumption that different levels of government are best able to make decisions for certain public responsibilities.

Remarkably, the neoliberal revolution has, in fact, weakened local and state government jurisdiction in order to make them subject to the whims of financial capitalism. But of far greater importance are the rules and policies that state and local governments make about infrastructure, education, and other services that create distinctiveness and build the long-run capacity of not only the local but synergistically the entire economy. It is easier for PE firms, and businesses in general, to comply with one set of national laws than to monitor the actions of fifty states and multiple municipalities, counties, and special districts. However, our argument is that local governments and communities are losing their freedom of action and ability to serve their constituents due to the passage of unnecessary national laws that preempt local laws better suited to the local context.

With fifty states, and so many counties and municipalities, we might expect to see great variation and policy experimentation. While this was the case earlier, the federal government regulatory agencies and courts have deliberately ruled in ways that inhibit and weaken state policy autonomy.

Return State & Local Autonomy: The Need to Limit Preemption

There is one organization and two forces that limit state and local autonomy. These would be an easy target for change. First, states have increasingly adopted uniform model legislation drafted by the American Legislative Exchange Council (ALEC), which is composed of conservative state legislators and executives from private companies that fund the organization. The second related force is preemption – a process by which state legislatures restrict the actions of smaller jurisdictions within their boundaries. We discuss each of these forces in turn.

ALEC is an organization founded in 1973 that actively promotes the neo-liberal agenda by proposing model legislation that limits the choices of state government. Rather than serious consideration of evidence of what is needed to promote the interest of citizens, ALEC creates model legislation that has been reproduced across states with conservative legislatures. The Center for Media and Democracy's website *ALEC Exposed,* monitors these activities. Most visible are efforts to limit gun control, and restrict abortion and civil rights, ALEC also promotes corporate interest over concerns about quality of life, with model legislation such as the Capital Gains Tax Elimination Act, that further advantages PE.[21] ALEC also has model legislation that limits states' ability to

---

[21] Wisconsin Governor Scott Walker made several changes to the state tax code drawn from ALEC corporate wish list. The budget bill excludes 100 percent of the capital gains realized on investments in Wisconsin for five years, costing Wisconsinites approximately $79 million per year, according to an analysis by the AFL-CIO. An additional exclusion from income tax for capital gains will amount to $36 million per budget cycle.

raise revenue, punishes socially responsible business practices, and restricts worker rights – all provisions that weaken opposition to PE takeovers.[22]

A second concern that is part of ALEC's agenda is preemption – the legal doctrine that allows state government to limit, or eliminate the power of municipalities to regulate a specific issue (Goodman et al., 2021). Consider the example of Wilson, North Carolina, a remote, low density that was unable to attract an Internet Service Provider (ISP). Taking initiative, the town champions organized their own broadband provider, Greenlight, as a local utility to provide reliable and affordable service, with free wireless in the downtown to attract visitors. Arguably, internet connectivity and broadband are essential services that are public utilities in the internet age that could be provided by a municipal government. But telecom companies enlisted the support of the North Carolina state legislature, who with the help of the ALEC, wrote legislation to restrict other jurisdictions from launching their own ISPs. Indeed, as of May 2023, sixteen states restrict municipal broadband networks. But laws can change: broadband preemption was eliminated in Maine, New York, and Colorado since 2022.

Reducing preemption at the city level would allow more flexibility and greater local regulation appropriate to the community. To address preemption, the National League of Cities (NLC) suggests a three-pronged response strategy to preemption that includes communicating the problems to local voters, forming citizens' coalitions to fight preemption, and using the court system to challenge state laws (Wagner et al., 2019). Swindell et al. (2018) add the use of ballot referenda to directly change states laws, and citizen lobbying of state legislature. These actions can be effective in addressing the range of restrictions, and requirements that limit local autonomy and ability to respond to the needs of local citizens.

Local and municipal activities are regulated by their state governments. State governments are responsible for laws and regulations that define how economic activity takes place, including regulating business activity, determining environmental standards, and overseeing labor practices. The federal government and, in particular, the judiciary and regulatory agencies have actively worked to erode this control to facilitate the free flow and operation of financial capital. State governments must be encouraged and protected when they assert their power to regulate their jurisdictions. While some might argue that this would erode the business climate the positive impacts on the quality of life of local residents would be apparent.

---

[22] The American City County Exchange (ACCE) is the sister organization that applies this model to city and county governments.

There are specific instances of what states can do. Muravchik and Shields (2023) provide a counterexample of the establishment wing of the Wyoming Republican Party that argues for focusing on the issues that state government can address, rather than discussing social issues that attract attention at the national level and galvanize voters. Often at the state level, the political parties can come to an agreement about budget and policy issues important to their citizens.

Cutting Off the Source – State and Local Pension Funds and Charitable Endowments

State and local government pension plans hold nearly $5 trillion in assets; their annual payments to beneficiaries are about 1.5 percent of the national GDP, with over 11 million beneficiaries relying on these plans to support their retirement (Sheiner, 2023). Public pension plans shifted away from fixed-income investments such as government and high-quality corporate bonds and turned to alternative investments such as PE in order to achieve their unrealistic investment return targets.

One of the most remarkable paradoxes of the entire PE industry is that it raises money from pension funds and charitable endowments. and issues will be whether to overturn the ability of public pension funds to invest in PE. The irony of public pension funds investing in organizations whose modus operandi is based on extracting value from the firms and even local governments that are the economic building blocks of local economies. There is now ample evidence that pension fund managers are not the "sophisticated investors" that the Securities and Exchange Commission (SEC) assumes them to be. The proliferation of fees and other charges levied on the portfolio firms and pocketed by the PE firm rather than flowing to the pension fund limited partners seems almost prima facie evidence of how they are out-classed by the PE firm managers. Additionally, the enormous amount of capital being deployed to the PE firms creates an enormous incentive for corruption on the part of the public pension fund executives. For example, in 2016, former CalPERS CEO Fred Buenrostro was sentenced to prison for guiding investment funds to Apollo Global Management and receiving kickbacks (US Department of Justice, 2016). Alternatively, when the PE portfolio does not perform well, state pension plans, despite their importance as general partners, have little recourse. In 2023, the PE firm, Blackstone, won a lawsuit against the Kentucky pension system, which claimed that the PE firm put the pension fund into unnecessarily risky investments (Paul Weiss, 2023). The lack of high returns promised by PE has likely prompted more litigation against PE firms but these are settled in mandatory arbitration. Unfortunately, the pension plans are unlikely to recover their losses given the way the legal system has been structured to favor PE.

State pension plans should be compelled to end their investment in PE – public pensions should not be participating in the destruction of their local economies. The realized returns are not better than safer investments, after management fees are taken into account (Phalippou, 2020). Alternatively, state and local pension funds could invest in companies and infrastructure projects in their own local jurisdictions (Clark, 1995), creating opportunity and igniting multiplier effects. This also solves an information problem as pension fund members would have more information on their investments and could be connected to local activity and frequent the firms where they have a stake.

The Role of States Attorneys Generals

In previous decades, state attorney generals reviewed acquisitions for antitrust implications (Ballou, 2023a, p. 238). In the process, the do-nothing Federal Trade Commission and Department of Justice never saw a merger they did not approve of decided to preempt smaller mergers, that is, exactly those that led to the roll-up of all manner of local government services. Empowering and encouraging the development of state antitrust regulators would ensure that smaller mergers that created local monopolies received greater scrutiny. State attorney generals can keep watch on PE firms' activities and acquisitions within their state and investigate any potential anticompetitive or antitrust violations.

State attorney generals can specifically investigate and take legal action against PE firms that engage in deceptive practices or anticompetitive behavior within their states. If there is evidence of fraudulent activities by PE firms operating within their states, state attorneys general can launch investigations and, if warranted, file civil or criminal charges against individuals or firms involved in the fraud. State attorneys general can collaborate with federal agencies like the SEC and the Department of Justice (DOJ) on investigations and enforcement actions involving PE firms that have a presence or operate within their states.

State attorney generals can enforce labor laws and protections to safeguard the rights and job security of workers and require PE to maintain existing collective bargaining agreements and ensure that employee compensation and benefits are not substantially reduced. Most states prohibit the corporate practice because the healing arts should not be transformed into a purely for-profit enterprise and, in our case, just an asset class to be monetized. PE firms have developed a variety of strategies to circumvent these laws (Zhu et al., 2023).

Congress should act to reinforce these laws and state governments should act to invalidate the strategies used to circumvent these laws. Such action would have significant benefits for communities particularly those that are under-served.

Most Americans agree that healthcare needs to be reformed. That important topic is certainly beyond the current volume. While our imagined ideal may be the decentralized healthcare system of the past, other solutions warrant consideration. One critical consideration is legislation or, at least, regulatory scrutiny to limit the roll-ups that allow PE to achieve a local monopoly position. Another concern is the impact on consumers, with two-thirds of personal bankruptcies in the United States related to medical debt (Himmelstein et al., 2019). The PE model is antithetical to providing high-quality, reasonably priced healthcare to Americans.

Legal action is another way to challenge PE. The PE firms have demonstrated that they will spend enormous amounts on advertising campaigns, consultant, and legal talent to defeat their opponents. This system is structured to operate against community and social welfare and in favor of extractive PE firms. A recent film, *Burial* (2023) dramatizes a David v. Goliath effort to limit the roll-up of funeral homes in Mississippi and exposes the predatory practices that made these acquisitions so profitable.

In many cases, there are laws preventing various PE practices but they are not enforced. Citizens should demand enforcement, both to improve medical care AND ensure that towns have medical practices that are local businesses embedded in their communities. Rather than the arms of anonymous PE firms that manage their practices by algorithm pressing their professional employees to constantly upsell patients and their families, there is a need to establish that access to healthcare is a fundamental human right, as established by the 1948 Universal Declaration of Human Rights

Greater Transparency & Oversight of PE Takeover Activity

States can adopt anti-takeover legislation, which can make it more difficult for PE firms to acquire or take control of companies based within the state. Karpoff & Wittry (2018) document that 43 states have enacted 153 anti-takeover laws. Guernsey et al. (2021) demonstrate that anti-takeover provisions benefit firms, specifically during the negative market shocks that attract PE.

Most of these provisions are designed for hostile, junk bond-funded, leveraged buyouts that were popular in the 1980s and 1990s. Laws can be updated to reflect the new PE reality of roll-ups and acquisitions. These laws often require shareholder approval for certain transactions or impose waiting periods. Two states (Massachusetts and Michigan) required tender periods of sixty days, which allows for public comment.

To limit the political influence of PE in the legislative process, states can enact campaign finance reforms, disclose political contributions, and regulate lobbying efforts. These measures can help reduce the ability of PE firms to shape legislation in their favor.

Limit corporate takeovers of essential public services

Approaches to preventing PE takeovers of public services will vary from one jurisdiction to another, and the success of these efforts depends on the specific legal and political landscape of the state. Collaboration among government agencies, lawmakers, community organizations, and concerned citizens is often key to achieving successful prevention of privatization when it is deemed not in the public interest. This would require transparency in the decision-making process regarding the potential privatization of public services. This would include disclosure of all relevant information, including financial terms, potential risks, and long-term consequences of privatization efforts. Such data would enable comprehensive economic and impact assessments before privatizing public services. Such assessments should consider the long-term financial implications and potential negative impacts on workers and service quality.

If local finances are strained and privatization can potentially be a viable option, contracts should include provisions in privatization contracts that establish performance standards, service quality benchmarks, and penalties for noncompliance. Contracts should also have clear exit strategies in case the private operator fails to meet its obligations. This should include long-term monitoring mechanisms for ongoing monitoring and evaluation of privatized services to ensure that they continue to meet public needs and expectations.

Remember that the approach to preventing PE takeovers of public services may vary from one jurisdiction to another, and the success of these efforts depends on the specific legal and political landscape of the state. Collaboration among government agencies, lawmakers, community organizations, and concerned citizens is often key to achieving successful prevention of privatization when it is deemed not in the public interest

Coupling Ownership with Responsibility

One of the most remarkable features of PE investing is the fact that the PE firm may own its portfolio firm, but legally the PE firm has no responsibility for the actions of the firm it owns. The PE firm appoints all of the managers and even because of its control of the board of directors makes policy but has no responsibility. Remarkably, if the portfolio firm commits fraud or borrows money to pay its PE owners a dividend and then goes bankrupt, neither the creditors nor the victims are able to claw back the payments. The quintessential example of this reported by Ballou (2023a) was of a patient at the second largest US nursing home chain, ManorCare, which had been acquired by Carlyle. In the transaction, ManorCare was loaded with so much debt that it was forced to cut back on costs causing health code violations to spike. As a result of the shoddy care, one patient fell and died and the family sued Carlyle, as, in the interim ManorCare had failed. The suit was dismissed after Carlyle argued that technically they were not the owner of ManorCare.

This decoupling of ownership and management responsibility is a powerful protection for the PE firm as it allows them to avoid legal/financial responsibility for the firms they own. An effective solution would be to mandate that PE firms accept responsibility for the actions of their portfolio firm. Effectively, since they own the portfolio firm, they bear responsibility for its actions and those wronged by the PE-owned firm should have the ability to sue the PE owner.

States can further impose regulatory requirements on PE firms, such as mandatory reporting, disclosure of fees and expenses, and transparency regarding their investment strategies. We have tried to demystify the PE model and more information helps ensure that the public has a clear understanding of PE operations.

New Types of Finance

Unfortunately, with the demise of community banking there are fewer financing options available to small businesses to finance expansion but also to provide lines-of-credit to smooth out fluctuations. Community banks engaged in relationship banking that relieves on soft information about lenders but has a greater understanding of the needs, and potential, of the local community. The reliance on soft information has been replaced by the credit score defined by an algorithm using standardized information. Those with a lower credit rating pay more in interest rates and have less access to opportunity, reinforcing their disadvantage and making it more difficult to reverse their fate.

Individuals who do not have access to a financial institution live in *Banking Deserts* and are forced to rely on payday lenders and others, which offer less favorable terms. Often, these same communities are also *Internet Deserts*, with less access to the high-speed internet required for Internet banking. For local businesses, there are limited places to deposit receipts, requiring travel and presenting a personal safety hazard.

Local ownership of small businesses, shops, and restaurants keeps profits local to be spent and invested in the community. Consider the case of the Green

Bay Packers, a major American football team that competes in the National Football League (NFL). The team's home of Green Bay, Wisconsin, stands as an outlier, as it is significantly smaller than most cities represented in the league. The Green Bay Packers have played in their original city longer than any other team in the NFL, despite being the smallest market in all of North America's professional sports. Green Bay was able to secure an NFL team and keep the team local because the Packers have been owned by a community-based corporation since 1923 (Feldman, 2018). No shareholder is allowed to own more than 200 shares, a safeguard to ensure that no one individual is able to assume control. The rewards are civic pride and the millions of dollars each game brings into the local economy. Interestingly, the NFL banned community ownership in 1960. While the Packers' ownership agreement was allowed, additional attempts to secure community ownership have not proceeded as the NFL has restricted other efforts at community ownership. Indeed, the NFL would like to allow PE to invest minority stakes in their teams, following practices in the National Basketball League (NBL), the National Hockey League (NHL), and the Major Soccer League (MSL).

Ownership Works, a nonprofit started by KKR veteran Pete Stavros, has experimented with employee ownership models in over sixty companies. Perhaps, not surprisingly, when workers are given an ownership stake, efficiencies increase, and the companies generate high rates of return. Workers receive compensation for their shares when the company is sold, which is an improvement in PE practices. Yet, the Ownership Works project is at risk of becoming a new form of corporate greenwashing – creating good feelings and a few social benefits while not addressing the systemic problem. Kelly & Kahn (2022) provide an illustrative example of how employee ownership could be used to protect workers and jobs, using contrasting examples of two guitar manufacturers. Gibson Guitars was taken over by KKR in 2018, while Taylor Guitars transitioned to 100 percent employee ownership in 2021. KKR incurred $250 million in new debt at Gibson, using $225 million for a special dividend to the PE fund, while announcing $7 million in profit sharing for Gibson's estimated 800 employees – about $9,000 each, with returns expected when the company is sold. In contrast, Taylor Guitars, by contrast, was bought out in a 10-year financing deal from a Canadian pension fund. The deal was structured as an employee stock ownership plan (ESOP), which are for-profit entities in which employees own part or all of the businesses for which they work. The Taylor deal did not saddle the company with excessive debt. Employees are motivated and will own the firm when the loan is paid off. The pension fund receives a good return, with no associated PE management fees.

There are 6,000 privately held companies, involving 2 million workers with ESOPS. The U.S. Department of Labor Employee Benefits Security Administration (EBSA) created a new Employee Ownership Initiative in 2023. EBSA will implement new programs to promote employee ownership and facilitate the formation of new programs, which may provide an alternative as companies undergo ownership changes. Educating consumers about how they vote their preferences when purchasing products will be part of making a change. We see this in *Buy Local* or *Buy American* campaigns but consideration of the ownership structure of the producing entity also matters.

These types of investment options are disdained by Wall Street but many small investors, who have not seen their portfolios grow are looking for alternatives. Another alternative financing is the *Slow Money* movement (Tasch, 2008). With various chapters around the United States, the organization acts as a match-maker between people who need small loans (typically for $5,000 or less at a rate of 2–3 percent) and people who would like to give loans. More than $80 million has been invested in over 1000 small food enterprises in the United States, with funds raised from 5,000 funders. Though this movement has focused on food and agriculture, its guiding principles can be applied to financing other types of small businesses that have a local, community focus. Michael Shuman (2020) provides advice for individuals to set up investments using Self-Directed IRAs and Solo 401(k)s to invest in local businesses. These investments offer opportunities for individuals to become engaged in their local communities, watch over their investments, and increase the local multipliers.

Responsible investment practices and preserving economic growth and innovation appear as a complex challenge. This requires creative new financing mechanisms, such as opportunities for worker buyouts and supporting institutions like community banks, credit unions, and co-ops. Encourage PE firms to engage in more responsible and sustainable investing practices. This can be done through incentives, tax breaks, or regulations that reward firms for socially responsible investments. And in even that PE cuts wages, and lay off employees, state and local governments can include *claw-back* provisions that would return public funds in the event of adverse outcomes.

PE goes international

Already in the 1980s, PE firms looked abroad for investment opportunities and, unsurprisingly, London became the European center for PE and initially, the UK absorbed much of the PE investment. However, as Christophers (2023) so ably shows, Europe and even the continent have become more PE friendly with largely the same results as in the US, though somewhat mitigated by a larger (though shrinking) public sector, regulatory and judiciaries that are not as dominated by neoliberals, and family-owned business in nations such as Germany that are not as eager to liquefy their operations. Despite these obstacles, in 2011 the European Union passed the Alternative Investment Fund Managers Directive which was meant to ensure greater transparency and require an independent valuation of the PE assets (Linklaters no date). While there have been some actions in Europe to rein in PE, in large measure, its activities go unchecked and unmonitored. Further, global financial institutions such as the International Monetary Fund and World Bank have deliberately encouraged the penetration of poorer nations by PE firms, thereby spreading the system to even more vulnerable nations that have weakly developed regulatory systems (Lerner et al., 2016).

Now is the Time to Act

Regardless of political party, all US citizens want a well-functioning economy and opportunities for themselves and their children. This is the essence of the American Dream that has been the social contract since the country's founding. There is now general dissatisfaction with the economy that is encouraging political unrest.

Neoliberalism and free market capitalism, with PE as the epitome, have created a society that is at odds with the type of future that most Americans want and without action now things will not get better. Rather than shrugging with hopelessness, focusing on national problems that are beyond their power to influence, or being diverted by the so-called culture wars, state and local government can embrace new ways of thinking that promote an equitable local future will prioritize economic development that benefits all residents, not just the extraction and transfer of value to a few financial centers. A more humane future would include supporting small businesses, promoting job training and education programs, and ensuring that economic opportunities are accessible to all. Communities should strive to ensure that there is quality of life and opportunity for residents.

Deciding on a future together is the essence of democracy. For the past forty, the government has been vilified as too large and ineffectual while business exerted political influence. What is needed is a re-balancing, adjusting the fulcrum so that the economy can thrive. Government, after all, most simply provides the rules in an economy, incentivizes good behaviors, and oversees the distribution of the returns. Many look to wealthy individuals, entrepreneurs, and tech millionaires to provide solutions and define the future but true change must come from consensus about the type of future our citizens want. The power to improve our future lies in our actions.

Our analysis highlights the changes that the operation of PE has induced over the past forty years. In reviewing the evidence, we became outraged at the extraction of value from American communities. Rather than making the US a better place, PE has enriched a few at the expense of most citizens, along the way dismantling communities by acquiring and looting local businesses and even public services. As the US economy has been degraded, PE is now looking for an international opportunity to export the worst of the US model of capitalism.

Capitalism will always require finance, which should be geared to investment in productive activity. The goal must be to increase the total value created not simply to extract value. This Element challenges us to refocus on rebuilding communities through long-term investment in citizens and public goods. PE, as it currently operates, cannot and will not provide results that lead to either greater efficiency or the achievement of other important social goals. It will only weaken our communities. This extractive financialized capitalism is contributing to an increasingly alienated population that believes that the system is corrupt and cares little about them. The future is ours to define – but we must act.

References

Abelson, R., & Creswell, J. (2012, August 14). A giant hospital chain is blazing a profit trail. *New York Times*.

Adler, L., Milhaupt, C., & Valdez, S. (2023). Measuring private equity penetration and consolidation in emergency medicine and anesthesiology. *Health Affairs Scholar*, *1*(1), 1–6.

Aghamolla, C., Jain, J., & Thakor, R. T. (2023). When private equity comes to town: The local economic consequences of rising healthcare costs. *SSRN*.

Alexander, B. (2017). *Glass House: The 1% Economy and the Shattering of the All-American Town*. St. Martin's Press.

Alonso, J. (2023, August 15). Rental increases are slowing down — Except in student housing. *Inside Higher Education*.

Americans for Financial Reform. (2022). Estimate of Private Equity Ownership of Housing Units. Research Memorandum to the House Financial Services Committee Members and Staff.

Appelbaum, E., & Batt, R. (2014). *Private Equity at Work: When Wall Street Manages Main Street*. Russell Sage Foundation.

Appelbaum, E., & Batt, R. (2019). Private equity and surprise medical billing. *Institute for New Economic Thinking*.

Appelbaum, E., & Batt, R. (2020, March). Private equity buyouts in healthcare: Who wins, who loses? Institute for New Economic Thinking Working Paper Series (CEPR Working Papers No.118). *Center for Economic and Policy Research*.

Ayash, B., & Rastad, M. (2021). Leveraged buyouts and financial distress. *Finance Research Letters*, *38*, 101452.

Bagdikian, B. H. (2000). *The Media Monopoly*. Beacon Press.

Baker, G. P. (1992). Beatrice: A study in the creation and destruction of value. *The Journal of Finance*, *47*(3), 1081–1119.

Baker, J. 2022. Testimony before June 28, 2022 Hearing of the U.S. House Committee on Financial Services, Subcommittee on Oversight and Investigations.www.congress.gov/117/meeting/house/114969/witnesses/HHRG-117-BA09-Wstate-BakerJ-20220628.pdf.

Ballou, B. (2023a). *Plunder: Private Equity's Plan to Pillage America*. Public Affairs.

Ballou, B. (2023b, April 25). Private equity is killing your pets. *Nation*.

Bank, S. A. (2014). Historical perspective on the corporate interest deduction. *Chapman Law Review*, *18*(1), 19–48.

Barber, F., & Gold, M. (2007). The strategic secret of private equity. *Harvard Business Review, 85*(9), 53–61.

Barth, J. R., Hamilton, P., & Markwardt, D. (2013). Where banks are few, payday lenders thrive. *White Paper, Milken Institute.*

Batt, R., & Appelbaum, E. (2018). Private equity pillage: Grocery stores and workers at risk. *The American Prospect.*

Bayliss, K., Van Waeyenberge, E., & Bowles, B. O. (2023). Private equity and the regulation of financialised infrastructure: The case of Macquarie in Britain's water and energy networks. *New Political Economy*, 28(2), 155–172.

Beck, T., Degryse, H., De Haas, R., & Van Horen, N. (2018). When arm's length is too far: Relationship banking over the credit cycle. *Journal of Financial Economics, 127*(1), 174–196.

Becker's Hospital Review. (2012, September 17). HCA shareholders allege Bain Capital and other private equity firms colluded in buyout.

Becker's Hospital Review. (2013, March 27). Private equity and non-profit hospitals: Strange bedfellows or saving grace?

Bel, G., Fageda, X., & Warner, M. E. (2010). Is private production of public services cheaper than public production? A meta-regression analysis of solid waste and water services. *Journal of Policy Analysis and Management, 29*(3), 553–577.

Bel, G., & Warner, M. (2008). Does privatization of solid waste and water services reduce costs? A review of empirical studies. *Resources, Conservation and Recycling, 52*(12), 1337–1348.

Berry, L. L., & Barauch, P. (2021, August 20). Hospital outsourcing often prioritizes profit over patients. *Texas A&M Today.*

Bivens, J., & Mishel, L. (2013). The pay of corporate executives and financial professionals as evidence of rents in top 1 percent incomes. *Journal of Economic Perspectives, 27*(3), 57–78.

Bivens, J. 2011. *Failure by Design: The Story Behind America's Broken Economy.* Washington, DC: Economic Policy Institute.

Bonvino, A., Ehrlich, A. J., Gonzalez, R. J. et al. (2021, October). False Claims Act & Qui Tam. *Paul Weiss.*

Bork, R. H. (1978). *The Antitrust Paradox: A Policy at War with Itself.* Free Press.

Borsa, A., Bejarano, G., Ellen, M., & Bruch, J. D. (2023). Evaluating trends in private equity ownership and impacts on health outcomes, costs, and quality: Systematic review. *BMJ, 382*, 1–17.

Braun, R. T., Jung, H. Y., Casalino, L. P., Myslinski, Z., & Unruh, M. A. (2021). Association of private equity investment in US nursing homes with the quality and cost of care for long-stay residents. *JAMA Health Forum, 2*(11), 1–13.

Bruch, J. D., Gondi, S., & Song, Z. (2020). Changes in hospital income, use, and quality associated with private equity acquisition. *JAMA Internal Medicine*, *180*(11), 1428–1435.

Bugbee, M. (2022, October 12). Profiting in Crisis: Exploring Private Equity's Investments in Travel Nursing Amidst a Critical Nursing Shortage and a Pandemic. *Private Equity Stakeholder Project*.

Burke, L. (2023, May 26). US veterans defrauded by for-profit universities fight to restore benefits. *Guardian*.

Burrough, B., & Helyar, J. (2010). *Barbarians at the Gate: The Fall of RJR Nabisco*. Random House.

Bykowicz, J. (2023, March 13). Barney Frank pushed to ease financial regulations after joining Signature Bank board. *Wall Street Journal*.

Cambridge Associates. (2021). *US Private Equity: Index and Selected Benchmark Statistics*.

Carroll, L. (2023, March 19). Practices are increasingly corporately owned, and pets owners pay the price. *Observer*.

Case, A., & Deaton, A. (2020). *Deaths of Despair and the Future of Capitalism*. Princeton University Press.

Cato Institute. (1985). New economic reasoning at the high court. *Regulation*.

Chetty, R., Hendren, N., Kline, P., & Saez, E. (2014). Where is the land of opportunity? The geography of intergenerational mobility in the United States. *Quarterly Journal of Economics*, *129*(4), 1553–1623.

Chhabra, K. R., McGuire, K., Sheetz, K. H. et al. (2020). Most patients undergoing ground and air ambulance transportation receive sizable out-of-network bills: An analysis of the prevalence and financial impact of out-of-network billing for ground and air ambulance transportation. *Health Affairs*, *39*(5), 777–782.

Chopra, R. (2018, July 24). Letter from Rohit Chopra, Commissioner of the Federal Trade Commission to Chairman Walden, Ranking Member Pallone, Chairman Harper, and Ranking Member DeGette of the House Energy and Commerce Committee, U.S. House of Representatives.

Christophers, B. (2023). *Our Lives in Their Portfolios: Why Asset Managers Own the World*. Verso Books.

Clark, G. (1995, December 10). Pension funds and urban investment: The design of alternative investment products. WPG96-1, *SSRN*.

Cobb, J. A. (2015). Risky business: Firms' shifting of retirement risk and the decline of defined benefit pension plans. *Organization Science*, *26*(5), 1332–1350.

Colburn, G., Walter, R. J., & Pfeiffer, D. (2021). Capitalizing on collapse: An analysis of institutional single-family rental investors. *Urban Affairs Review*, *57*(6), 1590–1625.

Davis, S. J., Haltiwanger, J., Handley, K. et al. (2021). The (heterogenous) economic effects of private equity buyouts (NBER Working Paper No. 26371). *National Bureau of Economic Research.*

Davis, G. F., & Kim, S. (2015). Financialization of the economy. *Annual Review of Sociology, 41,* 203–221.

Dorbian, I. (2017, September 14). Altaris Capital buys G&H Orthodontics from Riverside. *PE Hub.*

Douglass, E. (2017, July 8). Towns sell their public water systems – and come to regret it. *The Washington Post.*

Eason, B. (2023, February 16). American dream for rent: Investors slam tenants with fees, evictions. *The Atlanta Journal-Constitution.*

Easterbrook, F. H. (1984). Forward: The court and the economic system. *Harvard Law Review, 98*(1), 4–60.

Eaton, C., Howell, S. T., & Yannelis, C. (2020). When investor incentives and consumer interests diverge: Private equity in higher education. *Review of Financial Studies, 33*(9), 4024–4060.

Effinger, A. & Burton, K. (2014, May 10). Investors bet on trailer parks for double-wide returns. *Seattle Times.*

Eliason, P. J., Heebsh, B., League, R. J., McDevitt, R. C., & Roberts, J. W. (2022, February). The effect of bundled payments on provider behavior and patient outcomes: Evidence from the dialysis industry. Duke University Working Paper.

Ellen, I. G., & Dastrup, S. (2012). Housing and the great recession. *The Russell Sage Foundation & The Stanford Center on Poverty and Inequality.*

Ewens, M., Gupta, A., & Howell, S. T. (2022). Local journalism under private equity ownership (NBER Working Paper No. 29743). *National Bureau of Economic Research.*

EY. (2021). Economic contribution of the US private equity sector in 2020.

Fama, E. F., & Jensen, M. C. (1983). Separation of ownership and control. *Journal of Law and Economics, 26*(2), 301–325.

Federal Reserve System. (2022). *Profitability of credit card operations of depository institutions.* Board of Governors of the Federal Reserve System Report to Congress: July.

Feldman, M. (2018). Financing a future: Investing in communities and keeping profits local. *Società editrice il Mulino.*

Feldman, M., Guy, F., & Iammarino, S. (2021). Regional income disparities, monopoly and finance. *Cambridge Journal of Regions, Economy and Society, 14*(1), 25–49.

Fields, D. (2015). Contesting the financialization of urban space: Community organizations and the struggle to preserve affordable rental housing in New York City. *Journal of Urban Affairs, 37*(2), 144–165.

Fields, D. (2018). Constructing a new asset class: Property-led financial accumulation after the Crisis. *Economic Geography, 94*(2), 118–140.

Fields, D. (2022). Automated landlord: Digital technologies and post-crisis financial accumulation. *Environment and Planning A: Economy and Space, 54*(1), 160–181.

Fields, D., & Vergerio, M. (2022). Corporate landlords and market power: What does the single-family rental boom mean for our housing future? *UC Berkeley working paper.*

Fleischer, V. (2008). Two and Twenty: Taxing partnership profits in private equity funds. *New York University Law Review, 83*(1), 1–59.

Florida, R. L., & Kenney, M. (1988). Venture capital, high technology and regional development. *Regional Studies, 22*(1), 33–48.

Food & Water Watch. (2011). Selling Out Consumers: How Water Prices Increased after 10 of the Largest Water System Sales.

Friedman, M. (1970, September 13). A Friedman doctrine: The social responsibility of business is to increase its profits. *New York Times.*

Gallagher, C. (2023, August 23). Private equity on campus: Why college students are sleeping in cars. *Naked Capitalism.*

Gerstle, G. (2022). *The Rise and Fall of the Neoliberal Order: America and the World in the Free Market Era.* Oxford University Press.

Gillers, H. (2022, January 10). Retirement funds bet bigger on private equity. *Wall Street Journal.*

Goldstein, D. (2022, December 16). Can child care be a big business? Private equity thinks so. *New York Times.*

Goodman, C. B., Hatch, M. E., & McDonald III, B. D. (2021). State preemption of local laws: Origins and modern trends. *Perspectives on Public Management and Governance, 4*(2), 146–158.

Grant, M. (2013). Water privatization overview: Public interest perspective on for-profit, private sector provision of water and sewer services in the United States. *Journal of Law in Society, 14*(1), 167–192.

Guernsey, S., Sepe, S. M. & Serfling, M. (2021). Blood in the water: The value of antitakeover provisions during market shocks. *Journal of Financial Economics*, 1070–1090.

Gupta, A., Howell, S. T., Tannelis, C., & Gupta, A. (2021). Does private equity investment in healthcare benefit patient (NBER Working Paper Series). *National Bureau of Economic Research.*

Hall, P. A., & Thelen, K. (2009). Institutional change in varieties of capitalism. *Socio-Economic Review, 7*(1), 7–34.

Halleman, S. W. (2023, May 15). Envision healthcare files for chapter 11 bankruptcy. *HealthCareDive.*

Hamidi, S. (2020). Urban sprawl and the emergence of food deserts in the USA. *Urban Studies*, *57*(8), 1660–1675.

Hamlin, J. (2023a, March 31). Are private equity valuations too high – and would we know? *PitchBook*.

Hamlin, J. (2023b, January 10). "Warning signs': PE could impact public pension plans" funding status this year. *PitchBook*.

Haspel, E. (2023). Toddlers and investors aren't playmates: The threat of private equity in child care. *Capita*.

Hawryluk, M. (2022, September 22). Death is anything but a dying business as private equity cashes in. *KFF Health News*.

Himmelstein, D. U., Lawless, R. M., Thorne, D., Foohey, P., & Woolhandler, S. (2019). Medical bankruptcy: Still common despite the Affordable Care Act. American Journal of Public Health, *109*, 431–433.

Holland, M. (1989). *When the Machine Stopped: A Cautionary Tale from Industrial America*. Harvard Business School Press.

Hopkins, D. J. (2019). *The Increasingly United States: How and Why American Political Behavior Nationalized*. Chicago University Press.

Horowitz, J. M., Igielnik, R., & Kochhar, R. (2020, January). Trends in income and wealth inequality. *Pew Research Center.*Hospital Corporation of America. (2006). HCA enters into merger agreement with private equity consortium.

Ioramashvilli, C., Feldman, M. P., Guy, F., & Iammarino, S. (2023). Gathering round big tech: How monopoly, finance and start-up acquisitions reinforce US regional inequalities.

Ivory, D., Protess, B., & Bennet, K. (2016a, June 25). When you Dial 911 and Wall Street answers. *The New York Times*.

Ivory, D., Protess, B., & Palmer, G. (2016b, December 24). In American towns, private profits from public works. *New York Times*.

Jacobius, A. (2023, July 7). Private equity returns to fall below public index in 2023 – PitchBook. *Pension&Investments*.

Jarrell, G. A. (1983). State anti-takeover laws and the efficient allocation of corporate control: An economic analysis of Edgar v. MITE Corp. *Supreme Court Economic Review*, 2, 111–129.

Judge, B. (2023). Neoliberalism by Default: The Triumph of Finance Over Democracy. Ph.D. dissertation, *UC Berkeley*.

Kalleberg, A. L. (2000). Nonstandard employment relations: Part-time, temporary and contract work. *Annual Review of Sociology*, 26, 341–365.

Kamarck, E. C. & Gabriele, A. (2015, November 10). The news today: 7 trends in old and new media. *Center for Effective Public Management at Brookings*.

Kahn, L. (2024). Remarks by Chair Lina M. Khan As Prepared for Delivery Virtual Workshop on Private Equity in Health Care March 5, 2024. www.ftc .gov/system/files/ftc_gov/pdf/2024.03.05-chair-khan-remarks-at-the-virtual-workshop-on-private-equity-in-health-care.pdf.

Kaplan, S. (1989). Management buyouts: Evidence on taxes as a source of value. *Journal of Finance, 44*(3), 611–632.

Karpoff, J. M., & Wittry, M. D. (2018). Institutional and legal context in natural experiments: The case of state antitakeover laws. *Journal of Finance, 73*(2), 657–714.

Kelchen, R. (2017, January 11). How much do for-profit colleges rely on federal funds? *Brookings Institution.*

Kelly, M., & Kahn, K. (2022, May 19). Is private equity joining — or co-opting — the employee ownership movement? *Fast Company.*

Kelman, B., & Farmer, B. (2023, February 13). Doctors are disappearing from emergency rooms as hospitals look to cut costs. *KFF Health News.*

Kenney, M. (2011). How venture capital became a component of the US National System of Innovation. *Industrial and Corporate Change, 20*(6), 1677–1723.

Kenney, M., Bearson, D., & Zysman, J. (2021). The platform economy matures: Measuring pervasiveness and exploring power. *Socio-Economic Review, 19* (4), 1451–1483.

Kenney, M., & Zysman, J. (2016). The rise of the platform economy. *Issues in Science and Technology, 32*(3), 61–69.

KFF. (2009, March). National health insurance – A brief history of reform efforts in the U.S.

Kim, T. (2017, December 20). Gary Cohn: We 'tried 25 times' to cut hedge fund loophole in tax reform bill, but failed. *CNBC.*

Kingsolver, B. (2022). *Demon Copperhead.* Harper.

Kolhatkar, S. (2021, March 8). What happens when investment firms acquire trailer parks. *New Yorker.*

Krippner, G. R. (2005). The financialization of the American economy. *Socio-economic Review, 3*(2), 173–208.

Kuttner, R. (2022, January 14). Rollups: All monopolies are local. *The American Prospect.*

Lancieri, F., Posner, E. A., & Zingales, L. (2022). The Political Economy of the Decline of Antitrust Enforcement in the United States. Becker Friedman Institute Working Paper 2022–104.

Lapook, J., & Kaplan, M. (2022, December 6). What they've done is extremely evil: Pennsylvania hospital shutdown spurs questions about private equity in health care. *CBS News.*

Lazonick, W. (2023). *Investing in Innovation: Confronting Predatory Value Extraction in the US Corporation*. Cambridge University Press.

Lazonick, W., & O'Sullivan, M. (2000). Maximizing shareholder value: A new ideology for corporate governance. *Economy and Society, 29*(1), 13–35.

Lemann, N. (2000, June 5). No man's town. *The New Yorker, 5*, 42–48.

Lerner, J., Ledbetter, J., Speen, A., Leamon, A. N. N., & Allen, C. (2016). Private equity in emerging markets: Yesterday, today, and tomorrow. *Journal of Private Equity, 19*(3), 8–20.

Light, L. (2022, June 30). Private equity cashes in as student housing deals surge. *Chief Investment Officer*.

Malone, T. (2023, June 16). Residential real estate: Largest US asset class but not biggest economic driver. *Corelogic*.

Mann, C. L., & Warner, M. E. (2019). Power asymmetries and limits to eminent domain: The case of Missoula water's municipalization. *Water Alternatives, 12*(2), 725–737.

Markey, J., & Azorsky, G. (2023, May 9). Overlooked law states can use to get private equity out of health care decisions. *Law.com*.

Matthews, C. (2023, September 1). Private equity, hedge funds sue SEC over new disclosure rules. *MarketWatch*.

Mayer, R. M., & Beckel, M. (2009, November 23). Banking Committee Chairman Chris Dodd, a favorite of Wall Street, leads regulatory reform fight. *Open Secrets*.

McElhaney, A. (2022, December). Everyone wants to know what private assets are really worth. The truth: It's complicated. *Institutional Investor*.

McGuire Sponsel. (2022, April). Case Studies: Credits & Incentives G&H Orthodontics. *McGuire Sponsel*.

Melzer, B. (2011). The real costs of credit access: Evidence from the payday lending market. *The Quarterly Journal of Economics, 126*(1), 517–555.

Merme, V., Ahlers, R., & Gupta, J. (2014). Private equity, public affair: Hydropower financing in the Mekong Basin. *Global Environmental Change, 24*, 20–29.

Mesenbrink, J. (2023, May 25). Come on in, the water's warm: Private equity and other outside influences are entering the PHVAC market. But why? *Plumbing Perspective*.

Miller, H. (2022, October 28). Single-family home rentals and the rise of large landlords. *Investors Business Daily*.

Mishel, L. (2022, September 2). Growing inequalities, reflecting growing employer power, have generated a productivity–pay gap since 1979. *Economic Policy*.

Morgenson, G., & Rosner, J. (2023). *These Are the Plunderers*. Simon & Schuster.

Morse, A. (2011). Payday lenders: Heroes or villains? *Journal of Financial Economics, 102*(1), 28–44.

Muravchik, S., & Shields, J. A. (2023, September 7). Republicans in Wyoming see clearly what's happening. *New York Times.*

Nareit. (2021). The estimated total dollar value of commercial real estate was $20.7 trillion as of 2021: Q2.

National Research Council (2002). Privatization of water services in the United States: An assessment of issues and experience. The *National Academy Press.*

Nunn, R., Parsons, J., & Shambaugh, J. (2019). Nine facts about state and local policy. *Brookings.*

O'Grady, E. (2022). The Kids Are Not Alright: How Private Equity Profits Off of Behavioral Health Services for Vulnerable and At-Risk Youth. *Private Equity Stakeholder Project.*

Olbert, M., & Severin, P. H. (2023). Private equity and local public finances. *Journal of Accounting Research. 61*(4), 1313–1362.

Olson, L. K. (2022). *Ethically Challenged: Private Equity Storms US Health Care.* Johns Hopkins Press.

Office of Attorney General Maura Healey. (2021, October 14). *Private Equity Firm and Former Mental Health Center Executives Pay $25 Million Over Alleged False Claims Submitted for Unlicensed and Unsupervised Patient Care* [Press release].

Open Secrets. (2013, March). Contributors, Mitt Romney. *Open Secrets.*

Open Secrets. (n.d.). Search, Revolving door: Search database. *Open Secrets.*

Open Secrets. (2023a, March). Summary, Private equity & investment firms. *Open Secrets.*

Open Secrets. (2023b, March). Totals, private equity & investment firms. *Open Secrets.*

Oprysko, C. (2022, August). Who lobbies for carried interest backers. *Politico.*

Oreskes, N. & Conway, E.M. (2023). *The Big Myth: How American Business Taught Us to Loathe Government and Love the Free Market.* Bloomsbury.

Paul Weiss. (2023). Blackstone Wins Unanimous Appellate Victory in $50 Billion Action Brought by Kentucky Attorney General.

Pearl, R. (2023, February 20). Private equity and the monopolization of medical care. *Forbes.*

Phalippou, L. (2020). An inconvenient fact: Private equity returns & the billionaire factory. *Journal of Investing. 30*(1), 11–39.

Philippon, T. (2019). *The Great Reversal: How American Gave up on Free Markets.* Belknap Press.

Pierre-Louis Jr., W. (2023, January 12). How private equity amplifies the abuse of predatory lending. *Inequality.org.*

Press, E. (2023, June 15). The moral crisis of America's doctors. *New York Times*.

Prete, R. (2022, September 14). Got a pet? There's a good chance private equity backs your vet.

Private Equity Stakeholder Project. (2023). PESP Private Equity Hospital Tracker.

Protess, B., Silver-Greenberg, J., & Abrams, R. (July 14, 2016). How private equity found power and profit in state capitals. *The New York Times*.

Rafiel, Y. (2022, August 25). When private equity takes over a nursing home. *New Yorker*.

Reich, R. (1989, January 29). Leveraged buyouts: America pays the price. *New York Times*.

Richter, W. (2017, January 24). Financialization of rents gets taxpayer guarantees. *Wolf Street*.

Rodriguez-Pose, A. (2018). The revenge of the places that don't matter (and what to do about it). *Cambridge Journal of Regions, Economy and Society*, *11*(1), 189–209.

Sanger-Katz, M., Creswell, J., & Abelson, R. (2019, September 19). Mystery solved: Private-Equity-Backed firms are behind ad blitz on 'Surprise Billing'. *New York Times*.

Sasso, M. (2023, July 12).Why private equity is chasing plumbers and lumber yards. *Bloomberg News*.

Sayer, A. (2015). *Why We Can't Afford the Rich*. Policy Press.

Scheffler, R. M., Alexander, L., Fulton, B. D., Arnold, D. R., & Abdelhadi, O. A. (2023). Monetizing medicine: Private equity competition in physician practice markets. *American Antitrust Institute*.

Scheffler, R. M., Alexander, L. M., & Godwin, J. R. (2021). Soaring private equity investment in the healthcare sector: Consolidation accelerated, competition undermined, and patients at risk. *American Antitrust Institute*.

Schulte, F. (2022, November 14). Sick profit: Investigating private equity's stealthy takeover of health care across cities and specialties. *KFF Health News*.

Schultz, E. E .(2011). Retirement heist: How companies plunder and profit from the nest eggs of American workers. *Penguin Group*.

Scola, Nancy. (2012, April 14). Exposing ALEC: How conservative-backed state laws are all connected. *The Atlantic*.

Selbst, S. (2020). First circuit rules that Sun Capital Funds not part of "Controlled Group" and not liable for pension plan withdrawal liability. *Herrick*.

Sheiner, L. (2023). The sustainability of state & local pensions: A public finance approach, 23–8. *Center for Retirement Research at Boston College*.

Sherman, E. (2022, May 02). Are institutional investors helping sink the home market? *Globest.com.*

Shuman, M. (2020, June 17). In Print: Put Your Money Where Your Life Is: How to Invest Locally Using Self-Directed IRAs and Solo 401(k)s. *Stanford Lawyer.*

Slattery, C., & Zidar, O. (2020). Evaluating state and local business incentives. *Journal of Economic Perspectives, 34*(2), 90–118.

Sokol, D. D., Bensley, S., & Crook, M. (2020). Measuring the Antitrust Revolution. *The Antitrust Bulletin, 65*(4), 499–514.

Stegman, M. A. (2007). Payday lending. *Journal of Economic Perspectives, 21*(1), 169–190.

Sullivan, E. (2018). *Manufactured Insecurity: Mobile Home Parks and Americans' Tenuous Right to Place.* University of California Press.

Surowiecki, J. (2012). "Private Inequity", *The New Yorker.* January 22. www .newyorker.com/magazine/2012/01/30/private-inequity#:~:text=The%20real %20reason%20that%20we,the%20U.S.%20tax%20system%20works.

Swindell, D., Svara, J. H., & Stenberg, C. (2018). Local government options in the era of state preemption. *Local Government Review, 100*(6), 8–13.

Szpaller, K. (2021, December 23). City of Missoula loses "bad faith" claims in water case, may be on the hook for millions. *Daily Montanan.*

Tasch, W. (2008). *Inquiries into the Nature of Slow Money: Investing as if Food, Farms, and Fertility Mattered.* Chelsea Green.

Tkacik, M. (2022, November 4). The private equity guys trying to shoplift a supermarket chain before they sell it. *Slate.*

Toyou, D. D. (2018). Protection of private equity investors under the Dodd-Frank Act. *Journal of Law and Commerce, 37*(2), 115–166.

United States Government Accountability Office. (2019). Air Ambulance: Available Data Show Privately-Insured Patients Are at Financial Risk.

US Census Bureau. (2023, May 2023). Historical income tables: Income inequality. *US Census Bureau.*

US Department of Justice. (2016, May 31). Former CalPERS CEO Sentenced To 54 Months' Imprisonment for Role In Corruption Conspiracy.

US Department of the Treasury. (2022, December 6). Treasury announces seven additional states to receive up to $1.5 billion from U.S. Treasury Department to promote small business growth and entrepreneurship through the American Rescue Plan. *US Department of the Treasury.*

U.S. Securities and Exchange Commission. (2023, August 23). SEC Enhances the Regulation of Private Fund Advisers [Press release].

Vogell, H. (2022a, February 7). When private equity becomes your landlord. *Propublica.*

Vogell, H. (2022b, October 15). Rent going up? One company's algorithm could be why. *Propublica*.

Wagner, S., Davidson, N. M., Haddow, K. et al. (2019). Restoring city rights in an era of preemption: A municipal action guide. *National League of Cities*.

Wamhoff, S., & Hughes, J. (2022, December 6). Reversing the stricter limit on interest deductions: Another huge tax break for private equity. *Institute on Taxation and Economic Policy*. https://itep.org/reversing-the-stricter-limit-on-interest-deductions-another-huge-tax-break-for-private-equity/.

Warren, E. (2023). Private Equity: By the Numbers.

Webber, A. M. (1993). What's so new about the new economy? *Harvard Business Review, 71*(1), 24–33.

Weiser, M. (2017, December 20). Private no more: Montana city takes control of its water system. *New Humanitarian*.

Paul Weiss. (2023). Blackstone Wins Unanimous Appellate Victory in $50 Billion Action Brought by Kentucky Attorney General.

Whoriskey, P. (2018, July 1). "A way of monetizing poor people": How private equity firms make money offering loans to cash-strapped Americans. *The Washington Post*.

Wolfson, B. J. (2022, December 22). doctors call private equity staffing practices illegal and seek to ban them. *KFF Health News*.

Woodall, P., & Valdes-Viera, O. (2020). Double exposure: Retail workers hammered by combo crisis of pandemic and private equity. *Americans for Financial Reform Education Fund*.

World Population Review .(2023). Gini Coefficient by Country 2023.

Yamin, R. J. (1984). The Achilles heel of the takeover: Nature and scope of successor corporation products liability in asset acquisitions. *Harvard Journal of Law and Public Policy*, 7, 185–258.

Yong, S. (2023, February 24). Canada's $10-a-day daycare program: A guide for families. *MoneySense*.

Zeller, S. (2023). Essays on Healthcare, Households, and Firms. *New York University*.

Zessoules, D. (2022, April 25). Enduring lessons from the Pittsburgh & Flint water crises. *Demos*.

Zhu, J. M., Rooke-Ley, H., & Brown, E. F. (2023). A doctrine in name only-strengthening prohibitions against the corporate practice of medicine. *New England Journal of Medicine, 389* (11), 365–368.

Zorn, D., Dobbin, F., Dierkes, J., & Kwok, M. S. (2005). Managing investors: How financial markets reshaped the American firm. In Knorr-Cetina, K., & Preda, A. (Eds.), *The sociology of financial markets*, 269–289 . Oxford: Oxford University.

Acknowledgments

We would like to thank Arie Lewin and Till Talaulicar for this opportunity and for their encouragement. We also thank our families for their continuing and unwavering support. We would like to thank Gordon Clark, Frederick Guy and Simona Iammarino, William Lazonick, Mary Walshok, and John Zysman for comments and good conversations as this work developed. We appreciate the encouragement and suggestions of Arie Lewin and Till Talaulicar. Finally, we thank our families for their continuing and unwavering support.

Cambridge Elements ☰

Reinventing Capitalism

Arie Y. Lewin
Duke University

Arie Y. Lewin is Professor Emeritus of Strategy and International Business at Duke University, Fuqua School of Business. He is an Elected Fellow of the Academy of International Business and a Recipient of the Academy of Management inaugural Joanne Martin Trailblazer Award. Previously, he was Editor-in-Chief of *Management and Organization Review* (2015–2021) and the *Journal of International Business Studies* (2000–2007), founding Editor-in-Chief of *Organization Science* (1989–2007), and Convener of Organization Science Winter Conference (1990–2012). His research centers on studies of organizations' adaptation as co-evolutionary systems, the emergence of new organizational forms, and adaptive capabilities of innovating and imitating organizations. His current research focuses on de-globalization and decoupling, the Fourth Industrial Revolution, and the renewal of capitalism.

Till Talaulicar
University of Erfurt

Till Talaulicar holds the Chair of Organization and Management at the University of Erfurt where he is also the Dean of the Faculty of Economics, Law and Social Sciences. His main research expertise is in the areas of corporate governance and the responsibilities of the corporate sector in modern societies. Professor Talaulicar is Editor-in-Chief of Corporate Governance: An International Review, Senior Editor of Management and Organization Review and serves on the Editorial Board of Organization Science. Moreover, he has been Founding Member and Chairperson of the Board of the International Corporate Governance Society (2014–2020).

About the Series

This series seeks to feature explorations about the crisis of legitimacy facing capitalism today, including the increasing income and wealth gap, the decline of the middle class, threats to employment due to globalization and digitalization, undermined trust in institutions, discrimination against minorities, global poverty and pollution. Being grounded in a business and management perspective, the series incorporates contributions from multiple disciplines on the causes of the current crisis and potential solutions to renew capitalism.

Panmure House is the final and only remaining home of Adam Smith, Scottish philosopher and 'Father of modern economics.' Smith occupied the House between 1778 and 1790, during which time he completed the final editions of his master works: The Theory of Moral Sentiments and The Wealth of Nations. Other great luminaries and thinkers of the Scottish Enlightenment visited Smith regularly at the House across this period. Their mission is to provide a world-class twenty-first-century centre for social and economic debate and research, convening in the name of Adam Smith to effect positive change and forge global, future-focussed networks.

ADAM SMITH
PANMURE
HOUSE

Cambridge Elements ≡

Reinventing Capitalism

Elements in the Series

A full series listing is available at: www.cambridge.org/RECA

Printed in the United States
by Baker & Taylor Publisher Services